The Nonprofit Sector and the New Federal Budget

THE NONPROFIT SECTOR PROJECT

The Nonprofit Sector and the New Federal Budget

Alan J. Abramson Lester M. Salamon

THE URBAN INSTITUTE PRESS · WASHINGTON, D.C.

2100 M Street, N.W.
Washington, D.C. 20037

Printed in the United States of America
ISBN 87766-401-3

9 8 7 6 5 4 3 2 1

THE URBAN INSTITUTE is a nonprofit policy research and educational organization established in Washington, D.C., in 1968. Its staff investigates the social and economic problems confronting the nation and government policies and programs designed to alleviate such problems. The Institute disseminates significant findings of its research through the publications program of its Press. The Institute has two goals for work in each of its research areas: to help shape thinking about societal problems and efforts to solve them, and to improve government decisions and performance by providing better information and analytic tools.

Through work that ranges from broad conceptual studies to administrative and technical assistance, Institute researchers contribute to the stock of knowledge available to public officials and to private individuals and groups concerned with formulating and implementing more efficient and effective government policy.

THE NONPROFIT SECTOR PROJECT

Lester M. Salamon, Director

The Urban Institute's Nonprofit Sector Project is a broad-gauged inquiry into the scope and character of private, nonprofit organizations, and into the changing relationships between these organizations and government. The project involves several different types of analysis being conducted at the national level and in sixteen locales throughout the country. This report is one in a series of products of this project. A complete list of Nonprofit Sector Project publications is included in Appendix D of this report.

Support for this project has been made available by a wide cross-section of private funding sources including corporations, national foundations, and local or regional foundations throughout the country. A list of these sponsors is provided below.

Sponsors

Aetna Life & Casualty Foundation
Alcoa Foundation
Amoco Foundation, Inc.
The Atlanta Journal/ The Atlanta Constitution
Atlantic Richfield Foundation
AT&T Foundation
BankAmerica Foundation
The Buhl Foundation
The Bush Foundation
Carnegie Corporation of New York
Chemical Bank
Chevron, U.S.A., Inc.
The Chicago Community Trust
The Coca-Cola Company
Equitable Life Assurance Society
The First National Bank of Atlanta
The Flinn Foundation
The Ford Foundation
Gannett Foundation
The General Electric Foundation
General Mills Foundation
H.J. Heinz Company Foundation
Howard Heinz Endowment
Honeywell Foundation
Independent Sector
Richard King Mellon Foundation
Metropolitan Atlanta Community Foundation
Charles Stewart Mott Foundation
The Minneapolis Foundation
New York Telephone
The New York Community Trust
The Pittsburgh Foundation
PPG Industries Foundation
Prince Charitable Trusts
The Rhode Island Foundation
The Rockefeller Brothers Fund
The Rockefeller Foundation
The Saint Paul Foundation
The San Francisco Foundation
Shell Companies Foundation
United States Steel Foundation, Inc.
Wells Fargo Foundation
The Joseph B. Whitehead Foundation

CONTENTS

Page

APPENDIXES:

Page

TABLES

Page

FIGURES

Page

PREFACE

This report analyzes the impact of recent federal budget decisions and those proposed for the next three years on the thousands of organizations that make up the nation's private, nonprofit sector--that vast collection of hospitals, colleges, universities, day care centers, nursing homes, neighborhood organizations, advocacy groups, theater groups, art galleries, employment and training programs, social service agencies, health clinics, and many more.

Despite their importance, these organizations have tended to be ignored in both public policy debates and scholarly research. As a consequence, crucial features of their operations have not been well understood, including the extent to which government agencies have turned to nonprofit organizations to help deliver publicly financed services and the extent to which government budget decisions affect the revenues of these organizations as a result.

To remedy this situation, we issued a report in 1982 analyzing the potential impact on nonprofit organizations of the major federal budget changes proposed for 1982-85. The present report reviews what actually happened during this period to federal spending in fields where nonprofits are active, and to federal support of nonprofit organizations, and then assesses how the new proposals now being debated at the federal level would affect nonprofit organizations over the next few years.

In completing this report, we benefited greatly from the production and administrative support of Jacquelyn Perry and Jack Edwards, and from the computer assistance of George Chow and The Urban Institute Computer Services Department. Thanks are also due to The Urban Institute Press; to numerous public officials in executive branch agencies, in the Office of Management and Budget, in the Congressional Budget Office, and on a number of congressional committees; and to the funders of The Urban Institute Nonprofit Sector Project listed elsewhere in this report.

A.J.A.

L.M.S.

ABOUT THE AUTHORS

ALAN J. ABRAMSON is a research associate at The Urban Institute. He has also worked at the National Academy of Public Administration. Mr. Abramson received his M.A. and M.Phil. degrees in political science from Yale University, where he is working on his doctoral dissertation in political science. He earned his B.A. in government and psychology at Wesleyan University.

LESTER M. SALAMON is director of the Center for Governance and Management Research at The Urban Institute. Dr. Salamon has served as deputy associate director of the U.S. Office of Management and Budget and as professor of policy sciences at Duke University. The author of numerous books and articles on public policy issues, he earned his Ph.D. in government at Harvard University and his B.A. in economics and public affairs at Princeton University.

THE NONPROFIT SECTOR PROJECT

THE NONPROFIT SECTOR AND THE NEW FEDERAL BUDGET

by

Alan J. Abramson and Lester M. Salamon

SUMMARY OF PRINCIPAL FINDINGS

The reductions in federal spending recently proposed by the Reagan administration in its budget for federal fiscal years 1987-89 would place serious strains on the thousands of health clinics, day care centers, employment and training programs, social service providers, colleges, research institutes, neighborhood groups and other organizations that comprise the nation's private, nonprofit sector. What is more, these strains come on top of significant pressures already placed on these organizations as a consequence of the federal budget reductions that took place between 1981 and 1986.

These conclusions emerge from a detailed analysis of federal spending in fields where nonprofit organizations are active, and of federal reliance on nonprofit organizations to deliver public services in these fields. This analysis shows that the nonprofit sector plays a far more important role in American life than is often recognized and that an elaborate partnership exists between nonprofit organizations and government at all levels. As a consequence, reductions in federal spending not only place new demands on nonprofit providers operating in the same fields; they also threaten the revenues of these organizations and thus limit their ability to meet this demand.

In particular, an examination of recent federal spending changes and those proposed for 1987-89 under the three major alternatives being actively debated--the Reagan administration's proposed budget, the provisions embodied in the Gramm-Rudman-Hollings Balanced Budget and Emergency Deficit Control Act of 1985, and the budget resolution approved by the U.S. Senate in May 1986--reveals the following:

(1) Proposed Cuts in Fields Where Nonprofits Are Active. The Reagan administration's proposed budget for FY 1987-89 would reduce the value of federal spending in fields where nonprofit organizations are active, exclusive of Medicare and Medicaid, by a total of $78 billion below what would have existed had FY 1980 spending levels been maintained, a reduction of about $26 billion, or 25 percent, per year over this three-year period.

(2) Fields Most Severely Affected. These proposed cuts would fall most heavily on the fields of employment and training, where spending by FY 1989 would end up 73 percent below its FY 1980 level in inflation-adjusted terms; community development, where the reduction would be 66 percent; higher education (down 57 percent), health services (down 42 percent), social services (down 37 percent), and arts and culture (down 33 percent).

(3) Impact on Nonprofit Revenues. Because government has turned extensively to nonprofit organizations to deliver publicly funded services, these proposed changes would cut significantly into the revenues of many nonprofit organizations. In particular, outside of Medicare and Medicaid providers, private nonprofit organizations would lose a total of $22 billion in federal support between FY 1987 and FY 1989, a reduction of $7.4 billion, or over 40 percent, per year below what was available in FY 1980.

(4) Organizations Most Heavily Affected. These reductions would fall particularly sharply on community development organizations, which would end up with 71 percent less federal support than they had in FY 1980; social services organizations, which would lose 55 percent of their support; and higher education organizations, which would lose 55 percent of their support. These reductions are particularly significant in the case of the social service and community development organizations since federal support constitutes as much as half of their total revenues.

(5) Past Reductions in Federal Spending in Fields where Nonprofits Are Active. These proposed cuts come on top of prior reductions in federal spending in fields where nonprofits are active during FY 1982 through FY 1986. Compared to the levels that existed in FY 1980, the inflation-adjusted value of federal spending in these fields, exclusive of Medicare and Medicaid, declined by $70 billion during these five years. This represents reductions of about $14 billion, or 14 percent, per year, including a 2 percent reduction in FY 1986 associated with the first impacts of the Gramm-Rudman-Hollings Act. These already enacted cuts were concentrated in the fields of employment and training, social services, health services, community development, and higher education, with significant percentage declines also in the field of environment and conservation.

(6) Impact of Past Cuts on Nonprofit Providers. These reductions in federal spending in fields where nonprofits are active between FY 1982 and FY 1986 translated into revenue losses to nonprofit organizations, outside of Medicare and Medicaid, totalling $23 billion below what would have been available had FY 1980 spending levels been maintained. This represents a loss of approximately $4.6 billion in nonprofit revenues a year, or 27 percent of what was available outside of Medicare and Medicaid as of FY 1980.

These past cuts fell particularly sharply on community development organizations, which by FY 1986 will have lost 44 percent of the federal support they received in FY 1980; on social service organizations, which will have lost 40 percent of their federal support; on non-Medicare and Medicaid supported health service organizations, which experienced losses of 37 percent; and on arts and cultural organizations, which experienced reductions of 41 percent of their federal support.

(7) Private Giving and the Existing Funding Gap. Despite efforts to boost private giving in order to mitigate the effects of federal budget cuts, between FY 1982 and FY 1984 private giving was able to offset only about 7 percent of the overall reductions in federal spending in fields where nonprofits are active. In fact, private giving was only able to offset a quarter of the direct revenue losses sustained by private, nonprofit organizations during this period. Far from being able to expand their services to meet the increased demand left by government cutbacks, many nonprofit organizations consequently found it difficult to maintain even their prior level of services.

(8) Private Giving and the Future Funding Gap. To offset the overall reductions in federal spending in fields where nonprofits are active proposed in the president's latest budget, private

giving during FY 1987 through FY 1989 would have to grow at a rate seven to eight times higher than the peak rate it has achieved in recent years. Just to offset the direct revenue losses nonprofit organizations are projected to sustain during this period, private giving would have to grow at a rate that is two to three times higher than its recent peak rate.

(9) Gramm-Rudman-Hollings Act and the Senate Budget Resolution Versions of the FY 1987 Budget. Under the provisions of the Gramm-Rudman-Hollings Balanced Budget and Emergency Deficit Control Act of 1985, in the event the president and Congress fail to agree on a budget for FY 1987 that seems likely to bring the federal deficit close to $144 billion, automatic spending reductions are to be imposed on a broad array of defense and nondefense programs. Based on estimates developed by the Congressional Budget Office, these automatic cuts would reduce federal spending in fields of concern to nonprofits--outside of Medicare and Medicaid--about 89 percent as sharply as the president's budget proposal.

A third approach to the FY 1987 budget is embodied in the budget resolution approved by the Senate in May 1986. Under this proposal, defense spending would rise somewhat less extensively than under the administration's proposal and revenues would also increase somewhat. As a consequence, domestic programs would be cut less severely than under the administration proposal. For programs of interest to nonprofit organizations excluding Medicare and Medicaid, this proposed budget would thus yield spending cuts about 86 percent as severe as those in the president's budget.

(10) Scope of the Private Nonprofit Sector. Private, nonprofit service organizations, exclusive of churches, synagogues, and other sacramental religious congregations, had expenditures in 1980 of approximately $116.4 billion. This represented about 5 percent of the gross domestic product. Of this total, about 35 percent, or approximately $40 billion, came from federal program resources. By comparison, these organizations received approximately $26.8 billion in support from private charitable sources, including individuals, foundations, and corporations. Federal support thus outdistanced private charity as a source of nonprofit sector income by a factor of about 1.5 to 1.

Copies of The Nonprofit Sector and the New Federal Budget are available from The Urban Institute Press, P.O. Box 19958, Hampden Station, Baltimore, MD 21211 (301) 338-6951, for a cost of $10.00 plus $2.00 for shipping and handling.

CHAPTER 1

INTRODUCTION

The 1980s have been a period of considerable uncertainty for the thousands of family counseling centers, drug rehabilitation clinics, halfway houses, day-care centers, neighborhood organizations, advocacy groups, universities, research institutes, employment and training centers, social service agencies, nursing homes, and other organizations that comprise the nation's private, nonprofit sector.

Beginning in the late 1970s, and accelerating with the election of Ronald Reagan in 1980, major reductions occurred in federal spending in many of the fields where nonprofit organizations are active, and nonprofit organizations were called on to expand their services to fill the gap. Because a substantial share of the federal spending in these fields goes to support service provision by these same nonprofit groups, however, these cuts in federal spending also had the effect of reducing nonprofit revenues. Nonprofit organizations therefore found themselves caught in a squeeze--called on to expand their activities yet losing some of the resources they had available to support even prior service levels.

Because of congressional resistance to some of the cuts proposed by the president, the extent of this squeeze on nonprofits has been somewhat less severe than originally anticipated. Nevertheless, substantial real reductions did occur both in the levels of federal spending in many fields where nonprofits are active, and in the extent of federal support for nonprofit providers in these fields.[1]

Now major new pressures have arisen for further cuts in federal spending in these same fields to offset the massive deficits created by the administration's program of expanded defense spending and tax cuts, by the continued growth in entitlement spending, and by congressional unwillingness to endorse further domestic cuts. With the passage of the Gramm-Rudman-Hollings Balanced Budget and Emergency Deficit Control Act of 1985, Congress has committed itself, and the president, to the elimination of the federal deficit, in stages, by fiscal year (FY) 1991. In response, the Reagan administration has submitted a FY 1987 budget that would make further significant spending cuts in fields where nonprofits are active and, in turn, further reduce nonprofit revenues from federal sources.[2]

---

1. Both the original proposals and the developments through FY 1985 are analyzed in: Lester M. Salamon with Alan J. Abramson, The Federal Government and the Nonprofit Sector: Implications of the Reagan Budget Proposals (Washington, D.C.: The Urban Institute, 1981); Lester M. Salamon and Alan J. Abramson, The Federal Budget and the Nonprofit Sector (Washington, D.C.: The Urban Institute Press, 1982); Lester M. Salamon and Alan J. Abramson, "Nonprofits and the Federal Budget: Deeper Cuts Ahead," Foundation News (March/April 1985), pp. 48-54.

2. During 1984 and 1985, Congress and the president agreed to spending and revenue changes that have already shaved the projected FY 1987 deficit from $245.6 billion (as estimated in the administration's FY 1986 budget) to $181.8 billion (as estimated in the administration's FY 1987 budget). Under the Gramm-Rudman-Hollings Act, the FY 1987 deficit is supposed to be shaved another $38 billion, to $144 billion. This can be done either by reducing spending, increasing revenues, or a combination of the two.

For further detail on the Gramm-Rudman-Hollings Act, see chapter 6 and appendix A.

The purpose of this report is to analyze the potential impact of these new administration proposals on both the need for nonprofit services and on nonprofit receipts from the federal government during fiscal years 1987-89. To put these projections into context, however, the report also analyzes what has already happened to federal spending and federal support of nonprofits in these fields during FY 1982-85, and what is now projected for FY 1986 after taking account of the initial Gramm-Rudman-Hollings Act cuts that went into effect on March 1, 1986. Finally, the report compares what would happen to nonprofits under the proposed Reagan budget to what would happen to them in FY 1987 and beyond under two alternative approaches to dealing with the deficit--first, the provisions of the Gramm-Rudman-Hollings law; and second, the compromise budget resolution overwhelmingly endorsed by the Senate in May 1986.

Five questions thus form the heart of the analysis in the report:

1. How have the federal budget changes already enacted between FY 1982 and FY 1986 affected (1) overall federal spending in fields where nonprofit organizations are active, and (2) nonprofit revenues from the federal government in these fields?

2. What would be the potential effect on federal spending in these fields and on nonprofit revenues from federal sources of the new budget proposed by the Reagan administration for the period FY 1987 through FY 1989?

Throughout this analysis federal fiscal year (FY) data are used. The federal fiscal year begins on October 1 of each year and extends until September 30 of the subsequent year. Thus fiscal year 1987 begins on October 1, 1986, and ends on September 30, 1987.

3. To what extent has private giving managed to offset either the reduction in federal spending in fields where nonprofits are active or the losses in federal support to nonprofits that have already been sustained over the past several years? What rate of increase in private charitable giving would be needed to offset either the additional reductions in federal spending or the additional revenue losses to nonprofit organizations projected to result from the administration's budget proposals for FY 1987-89?

4. What difference would it make for nonprofit organizations if the automatic provisions of the Gramm-Rudman-Hollings bill or the budget plan embodied in the Senate's budget resolution of May 1986 were put into effect for fiscal year 1987 rather than the provisions of the Reagan administration's budget?

5, Given current deficit projections and political realities, what is the future likely to hold for federal spending in fields where nonprofits are active, and for federal support of nonprofits in these fields?

Structure of the Presentation

To answer these questions, the discussion here is divided into six chapters. The balance of this chapter reviews certain crucial features of our approach that must be understood to interpret the remainder of this report. Chapter 2 provides an overview of the nonprofit sector in order to set the stage for the budget analysis that follows. Chapter 3 then examines the first of the two major types of impacats of federal budget decisions on nonprofits that are of interest to us in this report--namely, their effect on the need for nonprofit services as reflected in overall changes in the levels of federal spending in fields where nonprofits are active. This chapter first reviews the changes that have already occurred in these spending levels between fiscal years 1982 and 1986 and then examines the changes proposed under the Reagan administration's budget for fiscal years 1987 through 1989. Chapter 4 then focuses on the second of the two major types of federal budget impacts on nonprofits--namely, their effect on the revenues of nonprofit agencies. Here, again, we look first at the changes that have already been enacted for the period FY 1982 through FY 1986 and then examine the changes projected under the administration's most recent budget for the FY 1987-89 period.

In chapter 5, we turn our attention from federal spending changes to the rate of growth in private giving needed to offset these two types of budget impacts on nonprofits. The chapter first explores the extent to which private giving has offset either of the two impacts of federal budget decisions over the past several years and then projects the rate of increase that would be needed to fill in for the federal cuts proposed in the administration's new budget. Finally, in chapter 6 we examine the potential implications for nonprofit organizations of the two alternative budget plans that have surfaced for FY 1987--first, the plan embodied in the Gramm-Rudman-Hollings Balanced Budget and Emergency Deficit Control Act of 1985; and second, the plan embodied in the "budget resolution" passed by the Senate in May 1986. In this chapter, we also speculate more generally on the likely scenario for budget developments of concern to nonprofits over the next year or so.

Key Features of the Approach

Before turning to the body of this analysis, it is important to identify a number of key features of our approach that affect the discussion throughout.

o **Focus on Programs of Concern to Nonprofit Organizations Only**

Although all federal activities can have some impact on private, nonprofit organizations, an attempt was made in this analysis to limit the focus to programs that have a significant impact either on the revenues of nonprofit agencies or on the demand for nonprofit services. In the first category are those programs that enlist nonprofits in the delivery of program services and reimburse them with public funds. The second category includes all the programs in this first category plus any other programs that deliver the kinds of services that nonprofits might reasonably be called on to provide if government involvement were to decline. As noted in more detail in chapter 3, about $150 billion in federal spending in FY 1980, out of a total federal budget of $591 billion--i.e., about 25 percent of the federal budget--falls into one of these two categories.

o **Focus on Both Demand and Revenue Effects**

Throughout this analysis, two types of budget-related impacts on nonprofit organizations are of interest. The first are impacts on the demand, or need, for nonprofit services, as measured by changes in the overall levels of federal spending in fields where nonprofits are active. The central notion here is that as federal spending in such fields declines, the need for services from private, nonprofit organizations increases. Indeed, it is precisely this substitution of private for public services that is a major objective of many of the cuts being proposed.

The second type of impact that is of interest is the effect that federal spending changes have on the revenues of nonprofit agencies. This impact results from the fact that nonprofit organizations are directly involved in the delivery of services in many federal programs and thus receive a significant share of their income from federal sources. As detailed more fully in chapter 4, of the $150 billion in federal spending on programs of interest to nonprofits in FY 1980, about $40 billion represented payments to nonprofit organizations to deliver federally financed services. As federal spending declines, therefore, so do the revenues of nonprofit agencies.

Since, in most federal programs, only a portion of the program's resources go to support nonprofit service delivery, the absolute size of the overall cuts in spending will obviously be greater than the absolute size of the revenue losses to nonprofit organizations. In other words, the latter are a subset of the former. But both are important as expressions of the impact of federal budget decisions on nonprofits.

- Focus on Outlays

Officially, when Congress enacts a budget it grants "budget authority," the authority to commit funds, to federal agencies. However, agencies are frequently unable to expend all of the funds available to them in the year for which the authority is given. Budget authority can therefore "carry over" from one year to the next.

Since our interest here is in the impact of budget decisions on actual nonprofit agency revenues and activity in a given year, budget authority is not the best measure to use. The more appropriate measure is "outlays," i.e. the amount of funds actually spent in a given year.

While outlays provide a clearer expression of federal activity in a given year, outlay projections are inevitably imprecise because it is difficult to estimate exactly what level of outlays will result in a particular year from a given level of budget authority. Nevertheless, outlays are a more useful measure of actual activity levels than budget authority. Throughout this report, therefore, all budget data will be expressed in terms of outlays. (For readers interested in a fuller discussion of these terms and of the budget process in general, a layman's guide to budgeting is provided in appendix A.)

- FY 1980 as the Baseline

Throughout this analysis, actual and projected spending levels are compared to those that actually existed in FY 1980, the year before the Reagan administration came to office. The one adjustment that is made is to convert outlays to "constant FY 1980 dollars" to take account of the effect of inflation on the value of the dollar and thus make the comparisons in the same terms.[3]

---

3. Conversion to constant FY 1980 dollars is accomplished by using the gross national product (GNP) implicit price deflator for all programs except health finance. For health finance, the deflator used

This approach differs from the one stipulated in the 1974 Budget and Impoundment Act, which calls on the Office of Management and Budget to compute a "current services budget" against which to compare proposed spending levels each year. The "current services budget" essentially spells out what the bundle of services provided by the federal government in a given year would cost in subsequent years taking account of inflation and other growth factors built into current law, but with no changes in existing policy. Proposed spending levels are then measured against this "current services" base.

The problem with this approach is that because policies have been changing dramatically in recent years, the current services budget is really a shifting target. Increases in spending over the current services level can still leave spending below a prior year's level if the current services budget already incorporates significant reductions from that prior year. The use of the actual spending levels at a given point in time avoids this problem. FY 1980 was chosen because it was the year before the Reagan administration came to power and yet it does not represent the high point of federal spending on many of the programs of interest to us here. In most of the social service programs, for example, the high point in real dollar terms occurred around FY 1977. For some of the health programs it occurred in FY 1981. The reductions reported here are therefore, if anything, slight understatements compared to what would be reported if another year had been used as the baseline.

- <u>Focus on Federal Resources and Actions Only</u>

  Many of the programs targeted for cuts in the administration's budget proposals involve matching relationships with state and local governments. No attempt is made here to calculate the state or local resources involved in these programs, however. Nor is any effort made to gauge how state and local governments have reacted or will react to federal cutbacks, whether they substitute state and local resources for lost federal revenues, maintain their existing levels of spending on these activities, or make similar cuts themselves. Finally, no

---

is the medical care component of the consumer price index. Actual deflators are used for FY 1981-85, and administration projections are used for FY 1986-89.

effort is made to assess whether state and local governments have altered or will alter their reliance on nonprofit organizations as a consequence of budget reductions. Rather, it is assumed that the mix between direct provision of services, contracting with for-profit providers, and contracting with nonprofit providers will remain the same in the foreseeable future as it has been in the recent past. Based on the analyses we have done at the state and local level, however, it is likely that this assumption understates somewhat the impact of proposed budget reductions on nonprofit providers.[4]

- No Assessment of the Merits of Budget Proposals or of Other Features of the Administration's Program

  The central purpose of the analysis presented here is to assess the implications of the administration's budget proposals, and of congressional action on these proposals to date, for nonprofit organizations and those they serve. No attempt is made here to evaluate the merits or drawbacks either of the administration's budget strategy

---

4. As part of The Urban Institute Nonprofit Sector Project, state and local spending and government reliance on nonprofits have been analyzed in sixteen local field sites. Initial results indicate some reduction in state/local spending on programs of interest to nonprofits in the early 1980s and some shifting of resources from nonprofit to for-profit providers. For further detail, see: Government Spending and the Nonprofit Sector in Cook County/ Chicago, by Kirsten A. Gronbjerg, James C. Musselwhite, Jr., and Lester M. Salamon (Washington, D.C.: The Urban Institute Press, 1984); Government Spending and the Nonprofit Sector in San Francisco, by Paul Harder, James C. Musselwhite, Jr., and Lester M. Salamon (Washington, D.C.: The Urban Institute Press, 1984); Government Spending and the Nonprofit Sector in Pittsburgh/Allegheny County, by James C. Musselwhite, Jr., Rosalyn B. Katz, and Lester M. Salamon (Washington, D.C.: The Urban Institute Press, 1985); Government Spending and the Nonprofit Sector in Atlanta/Fulton County, by James C. Musselwhite, Jr., Winsome Hawkins, and Lester M. Salamon (Washington, D.C.: The Urban Institute Press, 1985); Government Spending and the Nonprofit Sector in Two Arizona Communities: Phoenix/Maricopa County and Pinal County, by John S. Hall, James C. Musselwhite, Jr., Lori E. Marczak, and David Altheide (Washington, D.C.: An Urban Institute Research Report, 1985); and Government Spending and the Nonprofit Sector in Two Mississippi Communities: Jackson/Hinds County and Vicksburg/Warren County, by Stephen L. Rozman and James C. Musselwhite, Jr. (Washington, D.C.: An Urban Institute Research Report, 1985). For a fuller list of project publications, see appendix D.

as a whole, or of particular proposals. Such evaluations are important, but they lie beyond the scope of this report. Readers must therefore apply their own judgments about the strengths or weaknesses of particular programs and activities to the numbers provided here in order to reach a conclusion about whether these changes are, on balance, good or bad. By the same token, no attempt is made here to examine the likely effects on nonprofit organizations of other parts of the Reagan administration's program, such as the Tax Act of 1981.

- Use of Prevailing Economic Assumptions and Budget Projections

  Estimates about the policy and spending changes needed to achieve a given deficit target or spending level are heavily affected by the assumptions that are made about how the economy will perform. If interest rates are assumed to be high, for example, interest charges on the national debt will be high and sharper spending reductions will be required elsewhere in the budget to bring the deficit down to a given level. Any given budget therefore embodies a number of basic economic assumptions as well as a number of policy decisions about target spending levels.

  It is not our purpose here to evaluate the economic assumptions embodied in the president's budget or the alternatives. Rather, for most of this analysis we take these assumptions as given and ask what implications flow from the budget proposals built on them for nonprofit agencies.

Against the backdrop of these caveats then, how have the federal budget changes of the past several years affected nonprofit organizations, and what are the prospects for the years immediately ahead?

CHAPTER 2

WHAT IS THE NONPROFIT SECTOR?

In order to make sense of the impact that federal budget decisions have on the private, nonprofit sector, it is necessary to begin with a clear understanding of what this sector is, and of what portion of it is of concern to us here. This is particularly important in view of the general lack of attention that has been paid to this set of institutions in both public policy debates and academic research over the past several decades, and the considerable confusion that surrounds it as a consequence. Contributing to the confusion as well is the wide assortment of entities that qualify for tax-exempt or nonprofit status under United States tax laws. In fact, the Internal Revenue Code makes provision for over twenty different types of tax-exempt organizations, ranging from chambers of commerce to burial societies, from mutual insurance companies to community-based development organizations. Sorting out the organizations that are the appropriate concern of this report is therefore a major undertaking.

Types of Nonprofit Organizations

For our purposes here, three crucial dimensions of this range of organizations can usefully guide such a sorting-out process: first, whether the organization is essentially private-serving (i.e., focused on providing services to the organization's own members) or public-serving (i.e., focused on providing services to a broader public); second, whether the organization actually provides services or merely distributes funds to other service providers; and third, whether the services the organization provides are secular or sacramental and religious.

Based on these dimensions, it is possible to group most nonprofit organizations into four more or less distinct classes. The first are funding agencies, or fund-raising intermediaries, which exist not so much to deliver services as to channel resources to those who do. Included here are private foundations, United Way organizations, Blue Cross and Blue Shield, religious fund-raising federations, and the like. The second group of nonprofits are organizations that exist primarily to provide goods or services to their immediate members, rather than to society or the community at large. Included here are professional organizations (e.g., the bar associations), labor unions, trade associations, mutual insurance companies, and the like. The third are organizations that exist primarily to serve others, to provide goods or services to those in need or otherwise to contribute to the general welfare. Included here are educational institutions, cultural institutions, social welfare agencies, day care centers, nursing homes, hospitals, and the like. The fourth category embraces religious congregations or other organizations pursuing essentially sacramental religious functions.

Of these four types of nonprofit organizations, the ones of greatest concern to us here are those in the third group. These are the organizations most directly involved in delivering services that promote community welfare or serve broad public or educational purposes.[1] They are therefore the portion of the nonprofit sector that overlaps most closely with the purposes and functions of government. We will refer to these organizations as "public-benefit service organizations."

These public-benefit service organizations have long played a vital role in American life. They supply a considerable portion of the social services, health care, education, research, culture, community improvement, and public advocacy that occur in this country. In the process, they provide an important mechanism by which groups of citizens can band together in support of a wide variety of community purposes and a channel through which philanthropic impulses can be applied to worthwhile goals.

How Large Is the Nonprofit Service Sector?

Despite their importance, however, until recently we have known little about these organizations. To be sure, nonprofit organizations other than churches are required each year to file a special return (form 990) with the Internal Revenue Service listing all receipts as well as related financial data. Although portions of the resulting data

---

1. These organizations generally fall under two of the more than twenty sections of the Internal Revenue Code under which organizations can claim tax-exempt, or nonprofit, status: sections 501(c)(3) and 501(c)(4). These organizations are also the only ones eligible to receive tax-deductible gifts. However, these two sections also cover churches, foundations, and other fund-raising organizations that are not of concern here. Our focus, therefore, is on a subset of all 501(c)(3) and 501(c)(4) organizations--i.e., those that deliver services of a charitable, educational, or related character.

are extracted from these forms by the Internal Revenue Service and converted into data files, this process has gross imperfections that have impeded serious analysis. For one thing, there is considerable double counting because service providers and funding agents are grouped together in the data. A United Way grant to a nonprofit organization thus shows up twice, once as revenue for the United Way and once as revenue for the service organization. Although the Internal Revenue Service has an activity-code system that could be used to reduce this double counting, in practice the coding system is very flawed, and many organizations are coded incorrectly.[2] Beyond this, compliance with the reporting requirements is extremely uneven. Numerous organizations apparently do not file their forms, and others do so incorrectly. Finally, the information extracted from the forms by the Internal Revenue Service is minimal and does not include many data items needed to analyze agency finances with care.

Fortunately, a much more rigorous body of statistical data on the nonprofit sector became available in 1981 when the Census Bureau published the results of a special survey it conducted of tax-exempt service providers in 1977. Drawing on IRS lists of nonprofit organizations and other sources,[3] the Census Bureau made a serious effort to exclude

---

2. In the IRS data, for example, the Rockefeller Foundation is listed as a medical research institute instead of a foundation; the Carnegie Corporation is classified as an educational institution; and Loyola University of Chicago shows up as a church.

3. Chief among these was the list of organizations that had applied for exemption from payment of Social Security taxes, a privilege granted only to nonprofit firms.

funding organizations and eliminate double counting in the data it collected.[4]

By combining these two data sources, "aging" the census data to 1980 and adjusting the IRS data to exclude funding organizations and to take account of the miscoding of entries, we developed our own estimate of the size of the nonprofit sector as of 1980.[5]

---

4. Focusing on organizations with at least one paid employee, the Census survey identified 165,614 nonprofit service organizations as of 1977. Of these, 103,066 fall within the charitable, service-providing category of organizations of interest to us here. The remaining 62,548 organizations identified by the census survey included 23,418 labor unions, 1,123 political organizations, 16,618 business and professional associations, 7,386 other membership organizations, 446 business service organizations, 5,910 sports and recreation clubs, 3,096 organizational hotels and lodging houses, 826 sporting and recreational camps, and 3,725 other organizations. Taken together, the census identified $85.4 billion in expenditures by all nonprofit organizations as of 1977, of which $72.8 billion represented expenditures by what we have termed the public-benefit service portion of the nonprofit sector. See: U.S. Bureau of the Census, 1977 Census of Service Industries: Other Service Industries (January 1981). An update of this 1977 survey was conducted in 1982, but its coverage was far less complete.

5. The aging of the census data was done by assuming that all parts of the nonprofit sector other than the health care component grew at about the same rate as the gross domestic product, and that the health care component grew at about the same rate as overall health care expenditures. Because the large federal public sector employment program was created during this period and benefited nonprofits, a special modification was also introduced to accommodate it.

The IRS data were adjusted in three steps: First, using a tape of all 501(c)(3) and 501(c)(4) organizations provided by the IRS from its Exempt Organizations Master File, we deleted all organizations with activity codes suggesting they were not part of the charitable service component of the nonprofit sector of interest to us here. This adjustment reduced the total revenues of the sector from $215 billion on the raw IRS list to $174 billion, chiefly by deleting double counting. Second, to correct for miscoding among the remaining organizations, we examined the 500 largest organizations individually and deleted those that should have been coded in the excluded codes and shifted those that were appropriately included but in the wrong category. As it turned out, organizations representing another $38.8 billion in revenues that

The results of this analysis, reported in figure 1, indicate that the public-benefit service portion of the American nonprofit sector had expenditures in 1980 of approximately $116 billion. This represented about 5 percent of the gross domestic product. Quite clearly, this set of organizations represents a major economic force. In fact, at the local level, the nonprofit sector as defined here often exceeds local government in size. In the Pittsburgh metropolitan area, for example, the expenditures of private, nonprofit organizations exceed the total budget of the county government by a factor of six to one. In the Twin Cities area of Minnesota, the expenditures of the local nonprofit sector

---

should have been deleted were identified through this process; dropping them reduced the total revenues of the nonprofit sector from $174.1 billion to $135.3 billion.

Finally, a random sample of 1,000 organizations was selected from the overall IRS file and the activity-code listings for the entire file were adjusted in proportion to the miscoding found through an inspection of this random sample. For example, in our sample of 1,000 organizations, several large hospitals were found coded as educational institutions. To correct for this, an equivalent share of the total revenue of the set of organizations found in this activity code was allocated to the health care subsector. Similarly, numerous foundations, federated funding agents, Blue Cross organizations, business associations, and other organizations that lay outside our area of interest were discovered, and proportionate adjustments made to delete these from the overall totals as well. This final adjustment reduced the total revenues reported by another $6.7 billion, to $128.6 billion, which represents our best estimate of the size of the charitable and educational nonprofit service sector as it is portrayed in the IRS 990 data.

are as large as the combined budgets of the city of Minneapolis, the city of St. Paul, Hennepin County, and Ramsey County.[6]

These expenditures are not, of course, spread evenly among all types of nonprofit organizations. Rather, as figure 1 also shows, health organizations--mostly hospitals--accounted in 1980 for 60 percent of all nonprofit expenditures. Education organizations accounted for another 22 percent. This means that all the remaining types of nonprofit agencies--day-care centers, family counseling programs, neighborhood groups, advocacy organizations, arts agencies, and others--accounted for less than 20 percent of the total expenditures. Yet these organizations still represent a major presence in communities throughout the country. Quite clearly, the nonprofit sector has not withered away with the growth of government over the past several decades. To the contrary, this set of organizations remains a very vital force.

---

6. Michael Gutowski, Lester M. Salamon, and Karen Pittman, The Pittsburgh Nonprofit Sector in a Time of Government Retrenchment (Washington, D.C.: The Urban Institute Press, 1984); Barbara Lukermann, Madeleine Kimmich, and Lester M. Salamon, The Twin Cities Nonprofit Sector in a Time of Government Retrenchment (Washington, D.C.: The Urban Institute Press, 1984).

Figure 1
The Nonprofit Public-Benefit Service Sector, 1980
($ Billions)

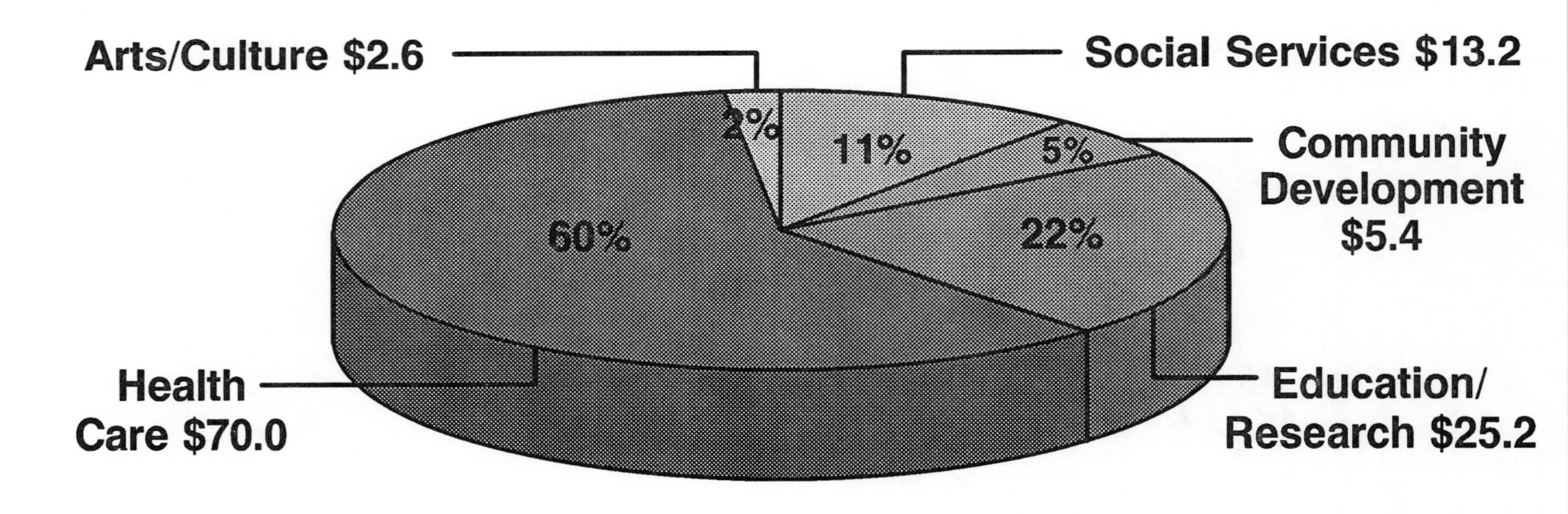

Total Expenditures $116.4

Source: Urban Institute Nonprofit Sector Project, Estimates Based on Census and Internal Revenue Data

The Private Philanthropic Base

While maintaining, and possibly expanding, its economic position, the nonprofit sector has experienced important changes in the composition of its revenues over the past several decades or more. In particular, the sector has gone well beyond its roots in private charitable giving. As noted in table 1, private giving, which embraces contributions or grants to charitable organizations by individuals, foundations, and corporations, totaled $49.1 billion in 1980, of which $22.3 billion went to churches and other religious congregations and $26.8 billion went to the service organizations of primary interest to us here. In other words, of the $116 billion in revenues received by nonreligious, nonprofit service providers in 1980, only 23 percent came from private giving. Even if religious organizations were included, moreover, the private philanthropic share of total nonprofit revenues would still not exceed 35 percent. In fact, these data on private giving probably overstate the extent of private support in the annual operating budgets of nonprofit organizations because they include contributions to endowments and gifts of appreciated assets like art collections that are not available for annual operating support.[7]

---

7. These data on the share of nonprofit income coming from private giving find confirmation in a survey we have done of some 3,400 nonprofit agencies exclusive of hospitals and higher education institutions. What these data reveal is that, as of 1981, private giving accounted, on average, for only 20 percent of the income of these agencies. By contrast, these agencies received 40 percent of their income from government and 28 percent from fees. For further detail see Lester M. Salamon, "Nonprofits: The Results Are Coming In," Foundation News (July/August 1984), pp. 16-23.

Table 1

Private Charitable Giving as a Share of Nonprofit Revenues, 1980
(Billions of Dollars unless Otherwise Indicated)

Type of Organization	Total Revenues	Private Giving	Private Giving as Percent of Total Revenues
Religious Congregations	$ 22.3	$22.3	100%
Service Providers	116.4	26.8	23
Total	$138.6	$49.1	35

SOURCES: Nonprofit revenues based on estimates developed from census and IRS data; data on private giving from Giving U.S.A., 1985 Annual Report (New York: American Association of Fund-Raising Counsel, 1985).

This limited reliance on private giving as a source of revenues is evident, moreover, in virtually all the major segments of the nonprofit sector. Although the data on private giving are not grouped exactly the same way as the overall revenue data and are somewhat overstated (because multiyear bequests and endowment contributions are included as if they were available for spending in the year in which they are made), it is still possible to shed some light on the extent of reliance on private giving by different types of nonprofit organizations if we compare our estimates of overall nonprofit revenues with the available data on private giving to different types of recipients. What emerges from such an analysis, as reflected in table 2, is that private giving constitutes less than half of the revenues of all types of nonprofit organizations except cultural organizations. In the case of cultural organizations the data on private giving are clearly inflated by the inclusion of multiyear bequests and endowments, as well as gifts of paintings and other artwork recorded at market value but not readily available for organizational support.

Table 2

Private Giving as a Share of Nonprofit Revenues, by Type of Organization, 1980 (Billions of Dollars unless Otherwise Indicated)

Type of Organization	Total Nonprofit Revenues	Private Giving	Private Giving as a Percent of Total Nonprofit Revenues
Social Service	$13.2	$ 5.0	38%
Community Development, Civic	5.4	1.5	28
Education/Research	25.2	6.9	27
Health Care	70.0	6.7	10
Arts/Culture	2.6	3.2[a]	a
Other[b]	--	3.5	--
Total	$116.4	$26.8	23%

SOURCES: See table 1.

a. Excess of private giving over total annual revenues of arts organizations reflects the inclusion of endowment contributions and the value of contributed artwork in the private giving data.

b. Other private giving includes a mix of organizations involved with foreign aid and technical assistance, international activities and education, and foundation endowment.

Summary

In short, the nonprofit sector remains a sizable and important component of American social and economic life. Embodying a distinctive national commitment to private action and voluntary association, nonprofit organizations have held their own in a shifting economic climate by taking full advantage of their distinctive base of private charitable support, but also by not being bound by it. In particular, nonprofit organizations have clearly developed other sources of financial support and formed supportive links with other sectors of American society. One of these routes of evolution has been in the direction of increased reliance on self-generated income from dues, fees, and sales. But equally important have been the relationships nonprofit organizations have established with government--relationships that are now very much under challenge. The remainder of this report will examine more closely the nature of these relationships between the nonprofit sector and government, and the impact on them of the major changes in federal policy that are now under way or under consideration.

CHAPTER 3

THE FEDERAL BUDGET AND THE NEED FOR NONPROFIT SERVICES

Federal budget decisions, as noted earlier, have two kinds of implications for private, nonprofit organizations. In the first place, they affect the need for nonprofit services by increasing or decreasing the resources that government is putting into certain kinds of activities. In the second place, they also affect the revenues of nonprofit agencies, and hence their ability to meet that need, since government is a significant funder of nonprofit organizations.

The purpose of this chapter is to analyze the effect of the budget decisions already implemented over the past five years, and those proposed by the Reagan administration over the next three years, on the first of these impact measures--namely, the need for nonprofit services. In particular, it examines what has happened to overall federal spending in fields where nonprofits are active between FY 1982 and FY 1986 and what further changes are proposed for FY 1987-89.

This range of impacts is important because one of the avowed objectives of the Reagan administration's budget policies over the past five years has been to shift more of the responsibility for addressing community needs from public to private institutions, among them private, nonprofit groups. Reflecting long-standing conservative beliefs, the administration has taken the view that a conflict exists between government and voluntary institutions and that the best way to aid the nonprofit sector is therefore to get government out of its way.[1] As President Reagan put it in a September 1981 speech, "The truth is that we've let government take away many of the things we once considered were really ours to do voluntarily...." Cutting back on government, in this view, is thus a way to stimulate voluntary action and open new opportunities for private, nonprofit institutions. Under these circumstances, it is important to understand the scale of the challenge thus being posed to the voluntary sector.

To do this, it was first necessary to identify the fields where both the federal government and nonprofit organizations are active and where the nonprofit sector could reasonably be expected to take up the slack left by governmental withdrawal. It was then necessary to determine the amount of federal spending in these fields as of FY 1980, and the extent to which this spending changed between FY 1982 and FY 1986. Finally, it was necessary to determine from the administration's latest

---

1. The origins of this line of thinking stretch back to conservative political philosophies of the late eighteenth century. This theory has taken on a modern flavor, however, in the works of sociologist Robert Nisbet, who has bemoaned the "decline of community" in the modern world, which he associates with the reduced hold of "intermediate associations" like the family, the church, the neighborhood, and the voluntary association, and which he attributes in large measure to the growth of government. As Nisbet puts it: "The conflict between the central power of the political state and the whole set of functions and authorities contained in church, family, gild, and local community has been, I believe, the main source of those dislocations of social structure and uprootings of status which lie behind the problem of community in our age.... The real conflict in modern political history has not been, as is so often stated, between state and individual, but between state and social group." See Robert Nisbet, Community and Power, 2d ed. (New York: Oxford University Press, 1962), p.268.

budget what further changes are now being proposed for the period FY 1987-89. The remainder of this chapter presents the results of this analysis.

Federal Activity in Fields in Which Nonprofits Are Active

Despite the diversity of the nonprofit sector and the considerable expansion in the range of federal government activities over the past several decades, the overlap between the nonprofit sector and the federal government is far from complete. Direct federal support in the field of religion, for example, is constitutionally proscribed; federal political advocacy is legally prohibited; and federal involvement in fields such as culture and the arts is relatively limited.

Nevertheless, there are at least seven major fields in which both the federal government and nonprofit organizations are both significantly involved: (1) social welfare, including social services, employment and training, and community development; (2) education and research, consisting of elementary and secondary education, higher education, and research and development; (3) health care, including health finance and health services; (4) income assistance, including housing, cash, food, and other income assistance programs; (5) international relief and assistance; (6) culture and the arts; and (7) conservation and the environment.

Within these fields, of course, the federal government and nonprofit organizations may do different things for different clienteles. A reduction in government activity therefore does not automatically translate into a need that the nonprofit sector could effectively or easily fill. Thus to go from a listing of fields of mutual interest to an assessment of the impact of budget cuts on the responsibilities of nonprofit organizations, it was necessary to identify the subset of programs in each field that are really relevant to the nonprofit organizations operating in them. Programs were included only if they met at least one of two criteria: (1) they provide revenues to nonprofit organizations, or (2) they provide services similar enough to those provided by nonprofit organizations that a change in program funding levels could reasonably be expected to affect the demand for services from some significant set of nonprofit institutions.

Following this rule enabled us to identify the programs of particular relevance to nonprofit organizations without including every domestic program in the federal inventory. For example, programs like Aid to Families with Dependent Children (AFDC); Food Stamps; Supplemental Security Income (SSI) for aged, blind, and disabled people; and other needs-tested income assistance programs were included since a reduction in their funding could be expected to translate into increased demands on nonprofit social service agencies. By contrast, the highway improvement and construction program was excluded because its funding level has limited influence on either the need for nonprofit services or the revenues of nonprofit organizations.

Using these criteria, we identified well over 100 federal programs of particular importance to the sector. As reflected in figure 2 and table 3, these programs accounted for over $150 billion in outlays in FY 1980.

Figure 2
Federal Outlays in Nonprofit Fields of Activity, FY 1980
($ Billions)

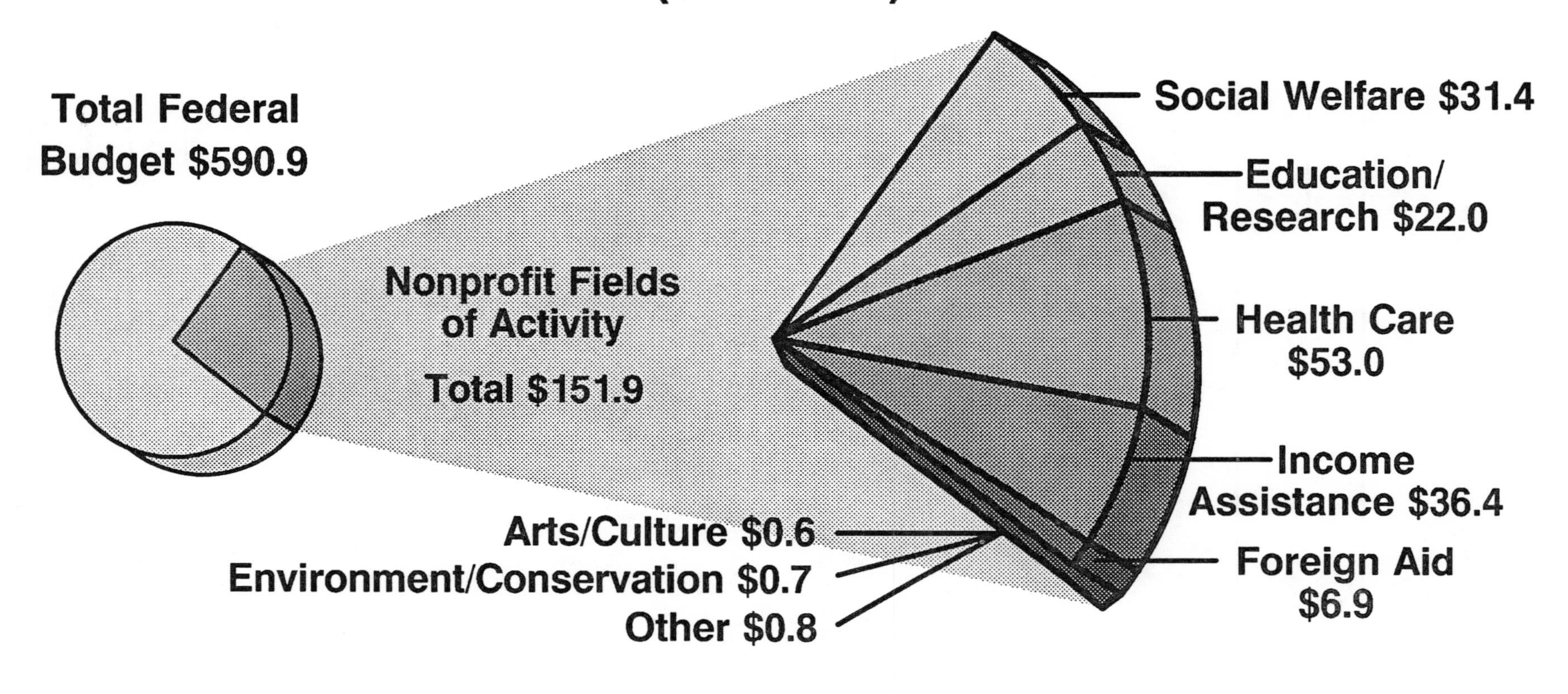

Source: The Urban Institute Nonprofit Sector Project, Adapted From U.S. Office of Management and Budget, <u>Budget of the United States Government, FY 1982</u>

Table 3

Federal Outlays in Programs in Which Nonprofits Are Active, FY 1980
(Billions of Dollars unless Otherwise Indicated)

Program Category and Subcategory[a]	FY 1980 Outlays	
	Amount	As a Percent of Total
Social Welfare	$ 31.4	20.7%
Social Service	7.3	4.8
Employment/Training	10.3	6.8
Community Development	13.7	9.0
Education/Research	22.0	14.5
Elementary/Secondary Education	7.0	4.6
Higher Education	10.4	6.8
Research/Development	4.7	3.1
Health Care	53.0	34.9
Medicare/Medicaid/Other Health Finance	49.7	32.7
Health Services	3.4	2.2
Income Assistance	36.4	24.0
Housing	5.5	3.6
Cash	14.7	9.7
Food	14.0	9.2
Other	2.2	1.4
Foreign Aid	6.9	4.6
Arts/Culture	0.6	0.4
Environment/Conservation	0.7	0.5
Other	0.8	0.5
Total	$151.9	100.0%

SOURCE: The Urban Institute Nonprofit Sector Project, based on data in Office of Management and Budget, Budget of the United States Government, FY 1982, unpublished backup material.

a. For further detail, see appendix B.

By comparison, total federal expenditures in that year amounted to $590 billion. In other words, the programs of interest to nonprofit organizations identified here represent slightly more than one-fourth of all federal expenditures.

Of this amount, by far the largest share, representing a third of all federal outlays in these fields, consisted of health care expenditures, chiefly for Medicare and Medicaid. Another one-fourth of the total represented income assistance payments. Spending for social welfare, and for education and research, accounted for about 20 and 15 percent of the total, respectively. Outlays for foreign aid, arts and culture, environment and conservation, and other programs (chiefly the nonprofit postal subsidy) made up the remaining 5 percent of federal spending in these areas.

Enacted Changes, FY 1982-86

Beginning shortly after it took office in 1981, and continuing every year after that, the Reagan administration sent budget proposals to Congress that called for deep reductions in federal spending in many of these fields of interest to nonprofits. Congress approved many of these proposed cuts in 1981, but generally refused to make significant additional cuts after that. What is more, in two areas, significant increases in spending occurred. In the first place, continued cost escalation and utilization substantially increased the levels of spending on the massive Medicare program, which provides reimbursements for medical care to the elderly. In the second place, the recession of 1982 increased income assistance expenditures despite efforts to limit eligibility under many of the needs-tested programs. Finally, in late 1985, faced with escalating deficits, Congress passed the Gramm-Rudman-Hollings (G-R-H) Balanced Budget and Emergency Deficit Control Act, which, among other things, mandated an initial round of across-the-board spending cuts that went into effect on March 1, 1986, for the 1986 fiscal year.

Aggregate Changes

The results of these developments are portrayed in figure 3. As this figure shows, total outlays on the programs of interest to nonprofits remained relatively close to their FY 1980 levels over the period FY 1982-86. However, this total figure obscures two quite different stories that are embodied in the data. The first is the story of Medicare, and, to a lesser extent, Medicaid. As shown in figure 3, Medicare and Medicaid spending grew steadily during this period, even after adjusting for inflation using a special health-cost deflator. By contrast, spending on the remaining programs of interest to nonprofits excluding Medicare and Medicaid declined significantly between FY 1981 and FY 1982 and then remained at this lower level over the subsequent four years, rising slightly between FY 1984 and FY 1985 but then dropping again between FY 1985 and FY 1986 as a result of the initial round of G-R-H cuts.

The scale of these changes is even more clearly evident in table 4, which records the year-to-year changes in federal spending for all programs of interest to nonprofits, for Medicare/Medicaid spending alone, and for all the programs excluding Medicare and Medicaid. As this table shows, by FY 1986, federal Medicare and Medicaid outlays will be 25 percent higher than they were in FY 1980, even after adjusting for inflation. By contrast, by the end of FY 1985 the inflation-adjusted value of federal spending on all other programs of concern to nonprofits was about 12 percent below its FY 1980 levels. Based on changes already enacted, including the initial round of Gramm-Rudman-Hollings cuts, this figure will drop an additional 2 percent by the end of FY 1986. Over this entire five year period, FY 1982-FY 1986, therefore, total federal spending on these programs will fall close to $70 billion below the levels that would have existed had FY 1980 spending levels been maintained. This represents an average reduction of about $14 billion a year below FY 1980 levels.

Figure 3
Changes in Federal Outlays in Nonprofit Fields of Activity*

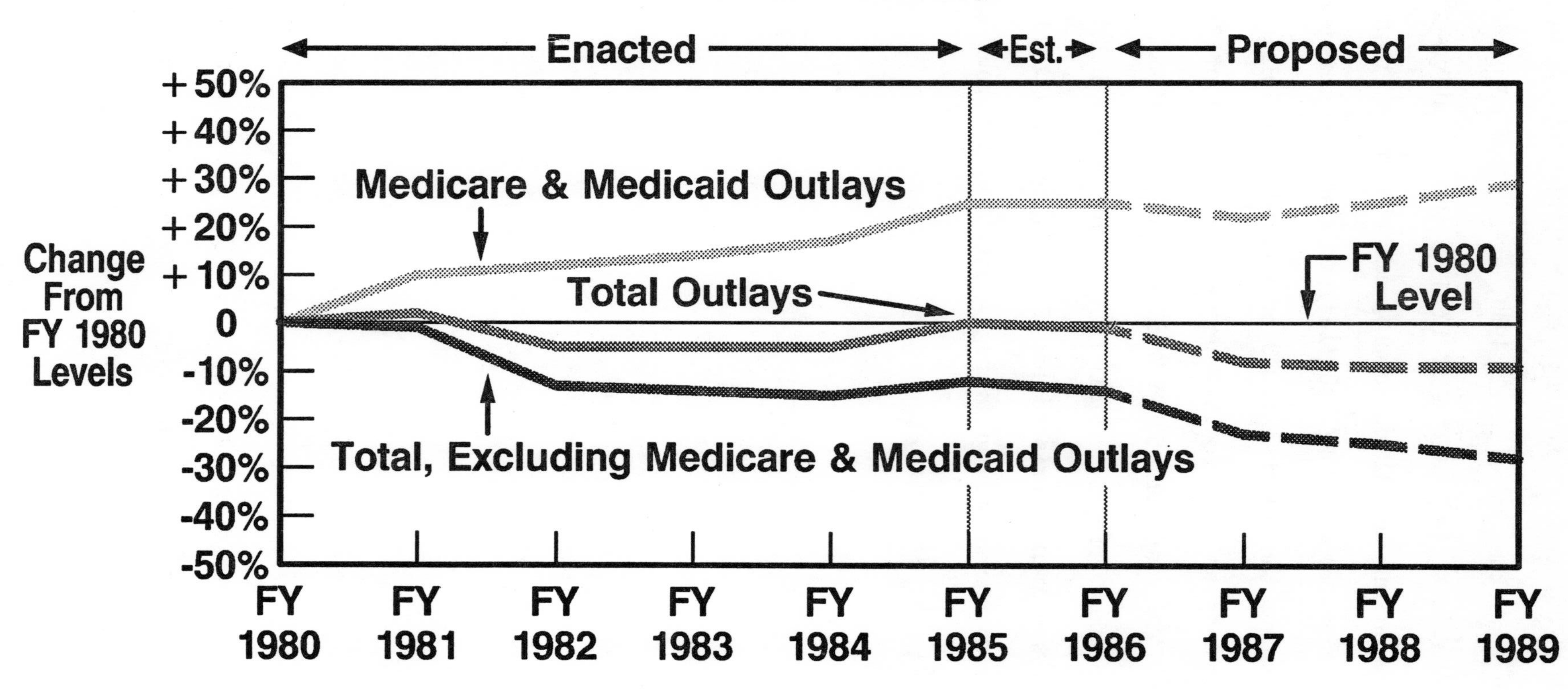

* Adjusted for Inflation

Source: The Urban Institute Nonprofit Sector Project, Adapted From OMB, Budget of the U.S. Government, FY 1987 and Preceding Years

Table 4

Past Changes in Federal Outlays in Programs in Which Nonprofits Are Active, FY 1980-86, in Constant FY 1980 Dollars (Billions of Dollars unless Otherwise Indicated)

Program Category	Actual						Estimated[a]	Total
	FY 1980	FY 1981	FY 1982	FY 1983	FY 1984	FY 1985	FY 1986	FY 1982-86
All Programs								
Outlays	$151.9	$155.4	$144.6	$144.3	$144.3	$152.2	$150.0	$735.3
Change from FY 1980								
Amount		+$3.5	-$7.3	-$7.6	-$7.6	+$0.3	-$1.9	-$24.1
Percentage		+2%	-5%	-5%	-5%	0%	-1%	-3%
Medicare, Medicaid								
Outlays	$ 49.1	$ 53.9	$ 55.0	$ 56.0	$ 57.3	$ 61.5	$ 61.1	$290.9
Change from FY 1980								
Amount		+$4.8	+$5.9	+$6.9	+$8.3	+$12.4	+$12.1	+$45.6
Percentage		+10%	+12%	+14%	+17%	+25%	+25%	+19%
Total, without Medicare, Medicaid								
Outlays	$102.8	$101.5	$ 89.6	$ 88.3	$ 87.0	$ 90.6	$ 88.8	$444.4
Change from FY 1980								
Amount		-$1.3	-$13.2	-$14.5	-$15.9	-$12.2	-$14.0	-$69.8
Percentage		-1%	-13%	-14%	-15%	-12%	-14%	-14%

SOURCE: The Urban Institute Nonprofit Sector Project, based on data in OMB, Budget, FY 1987 and preceding years, unpublished backup material.

a. Includes initial round of Gramm-Rudman-Hollings cuts, which went into effect on March 1, 1986.

Changes by Program Area

Even this breakdown of program categories fails to do justice to the pattern of change that occurred between FY 1982 and FY 1986. This is apparent in table 5, which records the year-to-year changes in federal spending in each of the major fields of concern to nonprofit organizations. As this table shows, there was considerable variation in the

Table 5

Past Changes in Federal Outlays in Programs in Which Nonprofits Are Active, FY 1982-86, in Constant FY 1980 Dollars
(Billions of Dollars unless Otherwise Indicated)

		Changes from FY 1980 Levels						Percent Change, FY 1986 vs. FY 1980
		Actual				Estimated	Total	
Program Category and Subcategory	FY 1980	FY 1982	FY 1983	FY 1984	FY 1985	FY 1986	FY 1982-86	
Social Welfare	$ 31.4	-$ 9.5	-$11.6	-$12.1	-$12.4	-$13.1	-$58.7	-42%
Social Services	7.3	-1.9	-2.0	-1.4	-1.9	-1.7	-8.9	-23
Employment/Training	10.3	-5.7	-6.0	-6.7	-6.5	-6.5	-31.5	-63
Community Development	13.7	-2.0	-3.5	-4.0	-3.9	-4.9	-18.3	-35
Education/Research	22.0	-2.7	-4.2	-4.8	-3.8	-4.0	-19.6	-18
Elementary/Secondary	7.0	-1.3	-1.9	-1.9	-1.2	-1.6	-7.8	-23
Higher Education	10.4	-1.4	-2.1	-3.1	-3.0	-3.1	-12.6	-29
Research/Development	4.7	-0.1	-0.2	+0.1	+0.4	+0.7	+0.9	+15
Health Care	53.0	+5.6	+6.1	+7.6	+11.6	+10.8	+41.8	+20
Health Finance	49.7	+6.1	+7.1	+8.6	+12.6	+11.9	+46.2	+24
Health Services	3.4	-0.5	-0.9	-1.0	-1.0	-1.1	-4.4	-32
Income Assistance	36.4	+0.4	+2.9	+2.3	+3.2	+3.5	+12.3	+10
Housing	5.5	+1.4	+2.2	+2.4	+3.1	+3.4	+12.4	+63
Cash	14.7	-0.4	+0.2	-0.2	+0.3	+0.7	+0.6	+5
Food	14.0	-0.8	+0.5	+0.1	-0.1	-0.4	-0.7	-3
Other	2.2	+0.3	+0.1	+0.1	-0.1	-0.3	+0.1	-13
Foreign Aid	6.9	-0.4	-0.2	+0.2	+2.2	+1.6	+3.3	+23
Arts/Culture	0.6	-0.1	-0.1	-0.1	-0.1	-0.1	-0.6	-15
Environment/Conservation	0.7	-0.3	-0.4	-0.4	-0.4	-0.5	-2.0	-70
Other	0.8	-0.1	-0.2	-0.1	-0.1	-0.2	-0.7	-27
Total	$151.9	-$ 7.3	-$ 7.6	-$ 7.6	+$ 0.3	-$ 1.9	-$24.1	-1
Total, excluding Medicare, Medicaid	$102.8	-$13.2	-$14.5	-$15.9	-$12.2	-$14.0	-$69.8	-14

SOURCE: The Urban Institute Nonprofit Sector Project, see table 4.

extent of the cuts among different program areas. The lion's share of the cuts were concentrated in the fields of social welfare and education/research, with substantial percentage declines in the environmental field as well. By contrast, substantial increases occurred in health care and income assistance, and to a lesser extent, in international assistance. The discussion below examines these changes in greater detail.[2]

Social welfare. Of all the program areas, the social welfare category absorbed the largest budget cuts between FY 1980 and FY 1985, the year just ended. During this period the value of federal spending in this area dropped from $31.4 billion a year to $19.0 billion, a decline of $12.4 billion or 39 percent, as shown in table 5. Between FY 1985 and FY 1986, spending in this field is projected to drop an additional 3 percent, to $18.4 billion. Altogether, therefore, the value of federal spending in this area will have declined by $58.7 billion over the entire five year period, FY 1982-86.

The largest portion of this reduction resulted from massive cuts in the federal employment and training programs beginning in FY 1982. Spending on these programs by FY 1986 was thus 63 percent below what it had been in FY 1980. Significant cuts also occurred in the fields of community development and social services. These cuts resulted from the following major changes that occurred in this field between FY 1982 and FY 1986:

---

2. For further detail on these changes, see the program-level data provided in appendix B. For a picture of these changes expressed in current dollars, before adjusting for inflation, see appendix C.

- o The elimination of the public service employment (PSE) program and the replacement of the Comprehensive Employment and Training Act (CETA) by the Job Training Partnership Act (JTPA), which was funded at a far lower amount.

- o Large inflation-adjusted cuts in spending for the Farmers Home Administration rural housing and rural development programs, for economic development assistance, and for the Community Development Block Grant program. Cuts in these community development programs are projected to be especially sharp between FY 1985 and FY 1986, reducing outlays in these programs by an additional 9 percent.

- o The creation of the Social Services Block Grant and Community Services Block Grant programs from preexisting programs, with funding at reduced levels, and with deep cuts as well in criminal justice assistance programs. While most social service programs sustained added cuts between FY 1985 and FY 1986 as a result of G-R-H and other factors (e.g., spending on the Social Services Block Grant will decline 8 percent in real terms between FY 1985 and FY 1986), in a few areas (e.g., foster care, rehabilitation services, and criminal justice assistance) increases occurred.

Education and research. Education and research programs absorbed the second largest cuts during the FY 1982-86 period, with reductions totaling $19.6 billion over the five years. Within this broad area, the reductions were concentrated in the subareas of higher education and elementary and secondary education. By contrast, spending for research grew slightly over the period. In particular:

- o In the field of higher education, Social Security adult student benefits were phased out; spending on veterans' educational benefits declined because of fewer eligibles; and Pell Grants and other campus-based student financial assistance were cut back substantially.

- o Despite a tightening of eligibility rules, federal outlays increased sharply for the student loan guarantee program because of the generally high prevailing interest rates that the government subsidized in the early 1980s, and because of the increased numbers of borrowers and higher default rates.

- Two elementary and secondary block grants were formed out of preexisting programs and funding was cut by over 30 percent. Impact aid and vocational and adult education programs were also cut by significant amounts.

- In the research area, Department of Defense research increased, while research spending by the National Aeronautics and Space Administration and the Environmental Protection Agency fell. Because the defense research increase was larger in absolute size, however, overall research spending increased.

Health. Largely as a result of increased spending for Medicare and Medicaid, federal health outlays rose substantially over the FY 1982-86 period. However, while Medicare and, to a lesser extent, Medicaid, spending increased, outlays for the smaller health services block grant programs (e.g., alcohol, drug abuse and mental health assistance; and preventive health services) declined significantly. In fact, by FY 1985 health services spending was 30 percent below FY 1980 levels. Between FY 1985 and FY 1986, spending on these services is projected to decline another 2 percent despite some restoration of earlier cuts in the preventive health services and maternal and child health block grant programs.

The most important changes in the health area consisted of the following:

- Massive growth in Medicare expenditures were seen despite limits on reimbursements to providers, the shift to a new prospective payment system, and the imposition of increased out-of-pocket charges on beneficiaries. This growth reflected the continued escalation of medical-care costs and the continued increase in utilization of Medicare-funded services.

- While Medicare spending increased considerably, spending on Medicaid, the health-care program for the poor, increased between FY 1980 and FY 1981 but then fell back to FY 1980 levels during FY 1982-84 before increasing slightly in FY 1985-86. These changes were a product of restraints on eligibility and reimbursement enacted in 1981 that led to reduced benefits and coverage.

- In the health services subarea, block grants were created and funding was cut for preventive health services; maternal and child health; alcohol, drug abuse, and mental health services; and primary care.

Income assistance. Like health programs, spending on income assistance also increased over the FY 1982-86 period. However, the 10 percent growth recorded in income assistance was concentrated almost exclusively in housing aid, where expenditures are driven by prior year commitments and changes in rent levels and housing costs. Cash, food, and other income assistance expenditures stayed just about even with inflation over the five year period. In particular:

- Supplemental Security Income (SSI) assistance for the aged, blind, and disabled; Food Stamps; food supplements for women, children, and infants (WIC); and refugee assistance all registered net increases over the FY 1982-86 period.
- By contrast, nutrition programs for children and others and the earned income tax credit dropped sharply, while low-income energy assistance and AFDC outlays fell slightly, despite the severe recession that occurred.

Foreign aid. Foreign aid programs also registered increased spending over FY 1982-86. By FY 1986, foreign aid outlays are projected to be 23 percent above FY 1980 levels after adjusting for inflation. However, the net rise in international assistance spending actually results from a mixture of increases and decreases in individual programs, including:

- o Sharp increases in the economic support program and in payments to multilateral development banks.
- o Cuts in refugee assistance abroad, in Public Law 480 food assistance, and in contributions to international organizations.

Arts and culture. Spending for arts and cultural activities declined by $580 million over the five years FY 1982-86, with the reductions concentrated in funding for the National Endowments for the Arts and Humanities and the Corporation for Public Broadcasting.

Environment and conservation. In percentage terms, environment and conservation programs of concern to nonprofits are projected to register the biggest drop of all program areas over the five years ending September 1986. By FY 1986 spending for these programs would be 70 percent below FY 1980 levels, resulting from declines in the federal land acquisition and historic preservation fund programs, and the complete elimination of the youth conservation corps.

Other--mail subsidy. In addition to the programmatic reductions noted above, reductions have also occurred in the mail subsidy provided to nonprofit, public, religious, and some for-profit organizations. By FY 1986, the value of this subsidy will have been reduced by some $200 million, or 27 percent.

The New Reagan Budget, FY 1987-89

Despite the spending reductions detailed above, the federal deficit skyrocketed between FY 1981 and FY 1985. This was so because the domestic spending reductions were swamped by a major increase in defense spending, by the effects of the 1981 tax cut, and by continued growth in the costs of entitlement programs such as Social Security and Medicare.

Although Congress made significant headway in reducing this deficit by boosting taxes and slowing the defense buildup during 1985, a sizable problem still remained as of late 1985, prompting Congress to enact the Gramm-Rudman-Hollings Balanced Budget and Emergency Deficit Control Act of 1985. As noted in chapter 1, this act sets rigid deficit targets for fiscal years 1986 through 1991 and stipulates that in the event the president and Congress fail to meet these targets across-the-board spending reductions will occur affecting defense and nondefense programs alike.[3]

The Reagan administration's budget for fiscal year 1987, unveiled in February 1986, proposes to meet these Gramm-Rudman-Hollings deficit targets, but in a way that avoids sacrificing either the administration's defense buildup or its program of tax cuts. To do so, the administration proposes further sharp reductions in federal spending in many of the programs of interest to nonprofit organizations. The remainder of this chapter examines how this proposed new budget would affect spending in fields where nonprofits are active over the three years FY 1987-89.

As reflected in the dotted lines on figure 3 above, the pattern of changes proposed for these three years closely resembles that imple-

---

3. Gramm-Rudman-Hollings sets a deficit target of $144 billion for FY 1987 declining to zero by FY 1991. By comparison, in the absence of further policy changes the FY 1987 deficit is projected to be $182 billion. Thus for FY 1987, G-R-H requires about $38 billion in deficit reductions. These targets are measured, however, against the "current services base," not last year's spending. For further detail on the G-R-H procedures, see appendix A.

mented over the past five years. In particular, despite some effort to restrain their growth, Medicare and, to a lesser extent, Medicaid spending would remain above their FY 1980 levels. Nevertheless, over the next three years total outlays on all programs of interest to nonprofits would decline. To achieve this, additional reductions below the already reduced FY 1985 spending levels are proposed for FY 1987 and subsequent years for the programs of interest to nonprofits outside of Medicare and Medicaid. In particular, these additional reductions total 12 percent for 1987, and 15 and 18 percent for FY 1988 and FY 1989, respectively. As shown in table 6, during FY 1987-89 federal spending in these fields would thus decline by a total of $78 billion below what it would have been had FY 1980 levels been maintained. This represents reductions of $26 billion a year, or about 25 percent, below what was available in FY 1980. By comparison, the reductions enacted during the previous five years averaged $14 billion a year below FY 1980 levels. In other words, the new budget would add an average of another $12 billion of cuts a year to the reductions already enacted as of FY 1986.

Table 6

Proposed Changes in Federal Outlays in Programs in Which Nonprofits Are Active, FY 1987-89 versus FY 1980, in Constant FY 1980 Dollars
(Billions of Dollars unless Otherwise Indicated)

Program Category	Actual		Proposed			Total
	FY 1980	FY 1985	FY 1987	FY 1988	FY 1989	FY 1987-89
All Programs						
Outlays	$151.9	$152.2	$139.1	$138.4	$137.7	$415.2
Change from FY 1980						
Amount		+$0.3	-$12.8	-$13.5	-$14.2	-$40.5
Percentage		0%	-8%	-9%	-9%	-9%
Medicare, Medicaid						
Outlays	$ 49.1	$ 61.5	$ 59.7	$ 61.2	$ 63.5	$184.4
Change from FY 1980						
Amount		+12.4	+$10.7	+$12.1	+$14.4	+$37.2
Percentage		+25%	+22%	+25%	+29%	+25%
Total, without Medicare, Medicaid						
Outlays	$102.8	$ 90.6	$ 79.4	$ 77.1	$ 74.2	$230.8
Change from FY 1980						
Amount		-$12.2	-$23.4	-$25.7	-$28.6	-$77.7
Percentage		-12%	-23%	-25%	-28%	-25%
Change from FY 1985			-12%	-15%	-18%	-15%

SOURCE: The Urban Institute Nonprofit Sector Project, based on data in OMB, Budget, FY 1987 and FY 1982, unpublished backup material.

Proposed Changes by Program Area

As detailed in table 7 and figure 4, the proposed cuts, like the ones already enacted, are concentrated in two fields: social welfare, including social services, employment and training, and community development; and education/research, particularly higher education. The discussion below details the proposed changes in the various fields.

Social services. In the social services field, federal outlays during FY 1987-89 would be $7.6 billion lower under the president's FY 1987 budget than if FY 1980 levels were still in effect, as indicated in table 7. By FY 1989, therefore, after adjusting for inflation, federal social service spending would be 37 percent below its FY 1980 level. This represents an additional 7 percent decline in FY 1987 below the already reduced level in the most recently completed fiscal year, FY 1985. The additional reductions result chiefly from the following proposed actions:

- Elimination of the community services, legal services, juvenile justice delinquency prevention, and housing counseling assistance programs.
- Consolidation of child abuse state grants and discretionary activities, and family violence services grants into a new Family Crisis and Protective Services Block Grant.

Figure 4
Enacted and Proposed Federal Spending Changes in Programs of Interest to Nonprofits, FY 1989 and FY 1985 Vs. FY 1980*

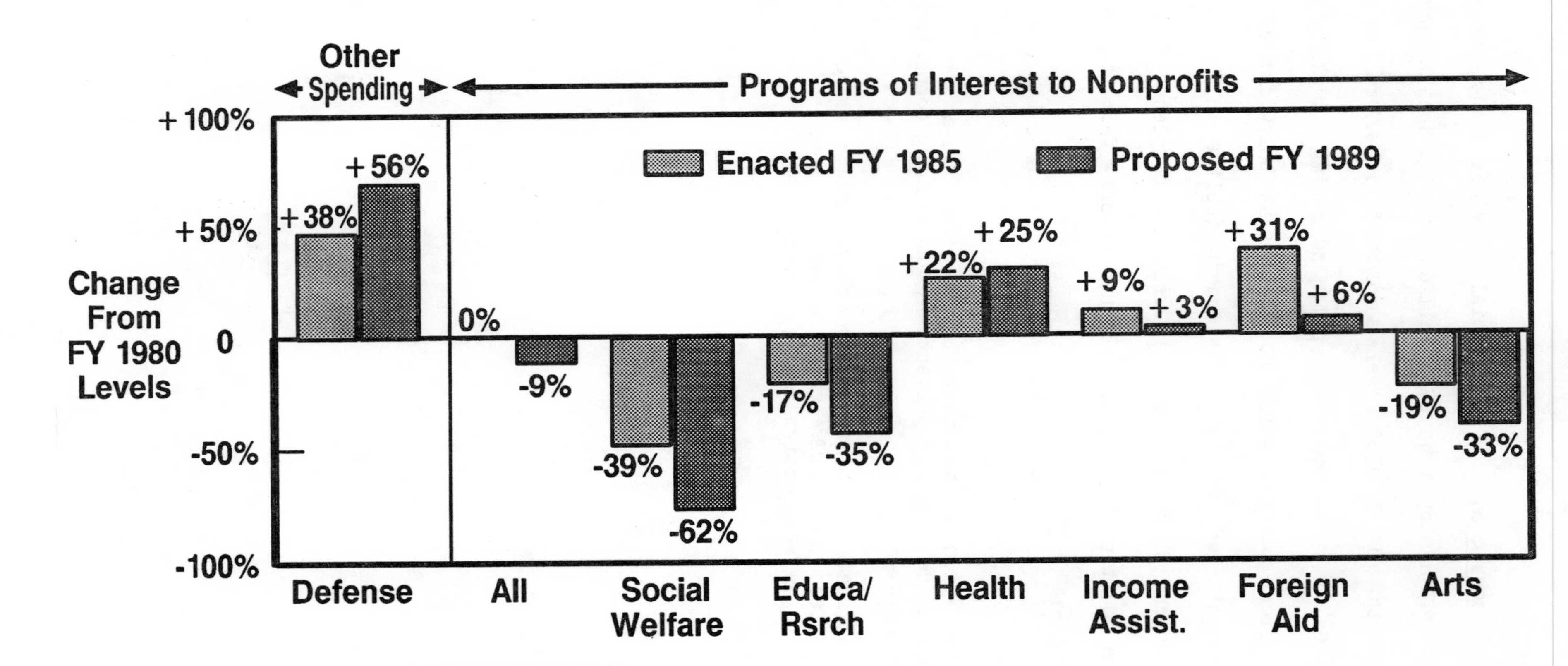

* Adjusted for Inflation

Source: The Urban Institute Nonprofit Sector Project, Adapted From OMB, Budget of the U.S. Government, FY 1987

Table 7

Proposed Changes in Federal Outlays in Programs in Which Nonprofits Are Active, FY 1987-89, in Constant FY 1980 Dollars
(Billions of Dollars unless Otherwise Indicated)

Program Category and Subcategory	Actual FY 1980	Changes from FY 1980 Levels					
			Proposed				Percent Change, FY 1989 vs. FY 1980
		FY 1985	FY 1987	FY 1988	FY 1989	Total, FY 1987-89	
Social Welfare	$ 31.4	-$12.4	-$16.7	-$18.2	-$19.4	-$54.2	-62%
Social Services	7.3	-1.9	-2.3	-2.6	-2.7	-7.6	-37
Employment/Training	10.3	-6.5	-7.2	-7.4	-7.5	-22.1	-73
Community Development	13.7	-3.9	-7.1	-8.2	-9.1	-24.4	-66
Education/Research	22.0	-3.8	-5.8	-7.1	-7.7	-20.5	-35
Elementary/Secondary	7.0	-1.2	-1.8	-2.0	-2.2	-6.0	-32
Higher Education	10.4	-3.0	-4.6	-5.8	-5.9	-16.3	-57
Research/Development	4.7	+0.4	+0.6	+0.6	+0.5	+1.7	+11
Health Care	53.0	+11.6	+9.2	+10.8	+13.0	+33.0	+25
Health Finance	49.7	+12.6	+10.5	+12.2	+14.4	+37.1	+29
Health Services	3.4	-1.0	-1.3	-1.3	-1.4	-4.1	-42
Income Assistance	36.4	+3.2	+1.1	+1.7	+1.1	+3.9	+3
Housing	5.5	+3.1	+3.0	+2.9	+3.0	+8.9	+55
Cash	14.7	+0.3	-0.2	+0.6	-0.1	+0.3	0
Food	14.0	-0.1	-1.3	-1.4	-1.4	-4.1	-10
Other	2.2	-0.1	-0.4	-0.4	-0.5	-1.2	-22
Foreign Aid	6.9	+2.2	+0.8	+0.7	+0.4	+2.0	+6
Arts/Culture	0.6	-0.1	-0.1	-0.2	-0.2	-0.5	-33
Environment	0.7	-0.4	-0.6	-0.7	-0.7	-1.9	-94
Other	0.8	-0.1	-0.8	-0.8	-0.8	-2.3	-100
Total	$151.9	+$0.3	-$12.8	-$13.5	-$14.2	-$40.5	-9
Total, excluding Medicare, Medicaid	$102.8	-$12.2	-$23.4	-$25.7	-$28.6	-$77.7	-28

SOURCE: The Urban Institute Nonprofit Sector Project, see table 6.

Employment and training. Federal employment and training programs, which sustained the largest reductions during the previous five years, are also hit hard by the new budget. In particular, the new budget would:

- Target youth employment programs for additional sharp reductions.
- Eliminate or replace the work incentive (WIN) and Veterans' Administration job training programs.
- Zero out the formula grant portion of the trade adjustment program, which provides help for workers who have lost their jobs because of changes in the economy.

Taken together these changes would reduce federal employment and training expenditures in FY 1987 another 17.5 percent below FY 1985 levels. By FY 1989, such expenditures would be 73 percent lower than they were in FY 1980.

Community development. Federal community development activities are the largest source of budget reductions under the new administration proposals, as indicated in table 7. Between FY 1985 and FY 1987 alone, these expenditures would drop another 33 percent. By FY 1989, therefore, outlays for community development programs under the new budget would be 66 percent below their FY 1980 level. The most important individual program changes proposed in the community development area involve:

- Further substantial reductions in the real value of resources committed to the Community Development Block Grant program.

- o Proposals to eliminate Urban Development Action Grants, the Farmers Home Administration rural development and rural housing activities, the Appalachian Regional Commission, the Economic Development Administration, and the emergency food and shelter program.
- o No new activity in the housing for elderly or handicapped program, in which nonprofits receive construction loans from the federal government.

Education and research. Total federal outlays for education and research would be more than $20.5 billion lower over FY 1987-89 under the president's budget than if FY 1980 levels had remained in place. Most of these cuts are concentrated in the higher education area, in which the real value of federal spending, which had already dropped from $10.4 billion in FY 1980 to $7.4 billion in FY 1985, would fall another 22 percent to $5.8 billion between FY 1985 and FY 1987. By FY 1989 federal higher education spending would end up at $4.4 billion, a decline of 57 percent compared to its 1980 level. However, the overall decline in the education and research area masks a mixture of cuts and some new initiatives. In particular, the new budget proposes to:

- o Tighten eligibility for student financial assistance and reduce outlays on health training and higher education institutional grants.
- o Create a new unsubsidized student loan program which would make repayments contingent on postgraduation ability to pay.
- o Substantially increase Department of Defense research and development outlays, reflecting the administration's strategic defense, or "Star Wars," initiative.

Health. Although health outlays are expected to remain well above their FY 1980 levels under the administration's new proposals, the new budget actually reduces health outlays from FY 1986 to FY 1987. Under the president's new budget:

- o Medicare reimbursements to hospitals and other providers would be cut with the result that real Medicare outlays would be reduced from FY 1986 to FY 1987, although they would rise again after that because of the expansion of the eligible population and of utilization rates. In addition, deductibles and premiums for Medicare recipients would rise.

- o Medicaid payments to states would be capped, and federal Medicaid outlays would decline in inflation-adjusted terms over the FY 1987-89 period. Medicaid expenditures would thus decline from 6 percent above FY 1980 levels in FY 1985 to 2 percent above FY 1980 levels in FY 1989.

- o The Primary Care Block Grant would be enlarged to include family planning and migrant health activities as well as health center funding, but spending by FY 1989 would be about 24 percent lower than FY 1980 spending on the equivalent programs.

Income assistance. Although the administration anticipates that income assistance expenditures will also remain above their FY 1980 level during the next three years, this is largely a result of past commitments under the housing programs. In its FY 1987 budget, the administration proposes to:

- o Make no new commitments for public or Indian housing units, although 50,000 additional households would receive housing vouchers.

- o Terminate the farm-labor housing, mutual and self-help housing, and nonprofit-sponsor housing assistance programs.

- o Require employable AFDC and Food Stamp recipients to work; penalize states for excess errors in their running of the AFDC and Food Stamp programs; and reform the method of federal reimbursement for state administrative costs in these programs.

Foreign aid. Foreign assistance spending would remain above FY 1980 levels during the FY 1987-89 period under the president's budget, as it was during the prior FY 1982-86 period. By FY 1989, foreign aid outlays are proposed to be 6 percent above FY 1980 levels. Among the individual program changes proposed in the president's new budget are these:

- o Reductions in Agency for International Development funding, Public Law 480 food assistance, and assistance to international organizations and conferences.
- o Continued real increases in the multilateral development assistance and foreign information and exchange programs.

Arts and culture. Arts and culture outlays, which declined 15 percent below FY 1980 levels as of FY 1986, would drop another 20 percent by FY 1989 under the administration's proposed budget. However, Smithsonian Institution activities would receive an initial real increase in funding, while other programs, including the activities of the National Endowments for the Arts and Humanities would be cut. As a result, by FY 1989, the value of federal support to the National Endowment for the Arts would be 38 percent below what it was in FY 1980; and for the National Endowment for the Humanities, it would be 51 percent lower.

The Institute of Museum Services is proposed for elimination in the new budget.

Environment and conservation. Federal spending on environment and conservation programs of interest to nonprofits would also continue to decline under the new budget. By FY 1989, spending on these programs would be 94 percent below FY 1980 levels. The new budget calls for the elimination of the urban park and recreation grant, historic preservation, and state outdoor recreation grant programs, and large reductions in outlays for federal land acquisition, including a three-year moratorium on new Forest Service land acquisition.

Other: the postal subsidy. One final major proposal in the president's new budget is to terminate the Treasury's reimbursement to the Postal Service for subsidized mail rates for eligible nonprofit and other organizations. As of FY 1980, this subsidy represented $753 million of expenditures in support of these agencies. The budget does indicate, however, that legislation will be proposed to allow the Postal Service to continue the subsidy on its own.

Summary

Between FY 1980 and FY 1986, significant reductions have thus occurred in the levels of federal spending in fields where private, nonprofit organizations are active, at least outside of health finance (Medicare and Medicaid). For the most part, these cuts occurred between FY 1981 and FY 1982, but they were then sustained, except for some modest reversals, over the ensuing three years and then deepened somewhat under the initial effects of Gramm-Rudman-Hollings. Although less severe than originally proposed, the cuts reduced the value of federal spending in these fields, after adjusting for inflation, by an average of $14 billion, or 14 percent, a year below what existed in FY 1980. In a number of these fields, however, the reductions were even deeper than this, dropping the value of federal support by 20 percent in the fields of social services and elementary education; by around 30 percent in the fields of higher education, health services, and community development; and by more than 60 percent in the fields of employment and training and environment.

Against the backdrop of these reductions already put in place, the president's new budget now proposes additional cuts in many of these same fields in order to meet the deficit targets of the Gramm-Rudman-Hollings Act while continuing the defense buildup. If enacted by Congress, this new budget would reduce the value of federal spending in fields where nonprofits are active, exclusive of Medicare and Medicaid, by an additional $12 billion a year over the three years FY 1987-89, bringing the total to an average of $26 billion, or 25 percent below what it was in FY 1980. For the three years as a whole, federal spending would thus be $78 billion less than it would have been had FY 1980 levels been maintained. As a consequence of these further cuts, by FY 1989 the inflation-adjusted value of federal support would drop below its FY 1980 level by over 30 percent in the field of arts and culture, by close to 40 percent in the fields of social services and health services, by close to 60 percent in the field of higher education, and by over 65 percent in the fields of community development, employment and training, and the environment. Here is a significant challenge indeed for the nation's private, nonprofit organizations.

The problem, however, is that the same government budget cuts that reduced the levels of government activity in these fields and thus increased the need for nonprofit services also reduced the resources available to nonprofit groups and thus their ability to meet this need. In point of fact, government and the nonprofit sector are not so much competitors in these fields as partners jointly serving community needs. To understand the full impact of the recent budget cuts and those proposed for the future on private, nonprofit organizations, therefore, it is necessary to turn from the present chapter's examination of changes in overall levels of federal spending in fields where nonprofits are active to a direct analysis of the implications of these changes for the revenues of the nonprofit agencies operating in these fields.

CHAPTER 4

THE FEDERAL BUDGET AND NONPROFIT REVENUES

Underlying many of the cuts in federal domestic spending in recent years is a body of conservative social theory that views government and voluntary organizations as natural antagonists and that supports government budget cuts as a way to strengthen the voluntary sector by getting government out of its way. In practice, however, the relationship between government and nonprofit institutions in this country is far different and far more complex than such theories acknowledge. While competing with nonprofit organizations in some areas, the federal government has also extensively underwritten their activities and stimulated the expansion and elaboration of their role.

Federal tax policy, for example, by exempting individual and corporate charitable contributions from taxation, effectively delivers an implicit subsidy to the sector. According to U.S. Treasury data, this subsidy was estimated to be worth $13.4 billion in FY 1985. As table 8 shows, about 10 percent of this implicit subsidy flows to the education component of the sector, about 12 percent to the health care component, and the remaining 78 percent to all other nonprofit organizations, including churches.

Even more important than these tax subsidies, however, are the direct programmatic resources that nonprofit organizations receive as a result of their participation in federal programs. The growth of federal activism, it turns out, has not involved simply an expansion of the federal bureaucracy and the displacement of nonprofit providers.

Table 8

Federal Tax Subsidies to Nonprofit Organizations through Deductibility of Charitable Contributions, FY 1985 (Billions of Dollars)

Type of Organization	Total: Amount	Total: As a Percent of Total	Source: Corporations	Source: Individuals
Education	$ 1.4	10%	$0.4	$ 1.0
Health	1.6	12	0.3	1.4
Other	10.4	78	0.5	9.9
Total	$13.4	100%	$1.2	$12.2

SOURCE: U.S. Office of Management and Budget, Budget of the U.S. Government, FY 1987, Special Analyses, pp. G-39, G-40.

Rather, the federal government has turned to a host of "third parties" to help it carry out its expanded responsibilities, and nonprofit organizations have figured prominently among them.[1]

In the process, an elaborate pattern of "nonprofit federalism" has taken shape linking governments at all levels to nonprofit organizations across a broad front. Far from being an alternative to or a competitor of nonprofit organizations, the federal government has emerged as a

---

1. For further elaboration of this point, see Lester M. Salamon, "Rethinking Public Management: Third-Party Government and the Changing Forms of Government Action," Public Policy, vol. 29, no. 3 (Summer 1981), pp. 255-275.

partner of these organizations, financing nonprofit operations, encouraging nonprofit involvement in new fields, and often helping to create new types of nonprofit entities where none had existed.

To be sure, these arrangements are not without their strains. Nonprofit organizations complain about excessive paperwork, insufficient provision for overhead costs, and burdensome regulatory requirements. Yet few doubt that, on balance, these relationships have been quite productive, providing needed resources for nonprofit action and creating a useful amalgam of public and private capabilities.[2]

Because of these relationships, however, the same budget reductions that place new demands on nonprofit organizations also reduce the revenues that nonprofits have available to meet these demands. To understand the impact on nonprofit organizations of the budget changes already enacted and the new changes now being proposed, therefore, it is important to look beyond the changes in the overall levels of federal spending in nonprofit fields of activity to examine in detail the direct implications of these changes for nonprofit revenues. To do so, this chapter is divided into three sections. The first section analyzes the origins and nature of federal support of nonprofit organizations and its extent as of FY 1980. The second section then examines the impact on

---

2. For a statement of the consensus view, see: Giving in America, Report of the Commission on Private Philanthropy and Public Needs (Washington, D.C.: U.S. Treasury, 1975). For a discussion of the theory of government-nonprofit relations, see: Lester M. Salamon, "Partners in Public Service: Toward a Theory of Government-Nonprofit Relations," in W. Powell, ed., The Handbook of Nonprofit Organizations (New Haven: Yale University Press, forthcoming 1986).

nonprofit revenues of the budget changes already enacted by Congress during the five years FY 1982-86. The final section considers the implications for federal support of nonprofits of the budget proposals recently advanced by the president for FY 1987-89. We will then turn in the following chapter to gauge the challenge that has been posed to private charitable giving by these federal cutbacks.

Nonprofit Federalism: The Background

Origins

Contrary to widespread belief, the involvement of nonprofit organizations with government is not a recent development in this country. To the contrary, it is rooted deeply in American history. In fact, some of this country's premier private, nonprofit institutions--such as Harvard University, Massachusetts General Hospital, the Metropolitan Museum of Art, and Columbia University--owe their origins and early sustenance to public sector support. As Waldemar Nielsen, the foremost student of this subject, has written:

> Through most of American history government has been an active partner and financier of the Third Sector to a much greater extent than is commonly recognized....Collaboration, not separation or antagonism, between government and the Third Sector (and the private economic sector as well) has been the predominant characteristic. Such

intimate association has also, on the whole, proven to be highly productive....[3]

Although the partnership between government and the nonprofit sector has deep roots in American history, it has expanded in both scope and scale in recent decades. What is more, it has taken new and more elaborate form with the emergence of the federal government as a key participant in the funding and support of nonprofit action.

Typical of these developments has been the evolution of the mixed economy of social services. Prior to the 1960s, the provision of social services was a shared responsibility of the voluntary sector and state or local governments. State activities throughout much of the nineteenth century focused on the development of institutions for the care of deaf, blind, and mentally or physically handicapped persons, while private agencies handled home care and various forms of direct assistance. As state and local involvement in the social services field expanded during the Progressive era at the turn of the century, however, it was accompanied by an increased flow of public funds to voluntary agencies to provide a broader range of services. In the process, a significant pattern of government-nonprofit partnership began to take shape to cope with the nation's social service needs. Thus, by the 1890s half of the government spending in support of the poor in New York

---

3. Waldemar Nielsen, The Endangered Sector (New York: Columbia University Press, 1980), pp. 14, 47.

City was channelled through private, voluntary agencies that delivered the services financed by public funds.[4]

Although the federal government entered the social welfare field in the 1930s, in the three decades that followed Washington concentrated almost exclusively on providing financial support to state and local governments to help them support their cash assistance programs for orphans, disabled persons, and the needy elderly. Not until the early 1960s did the federal government become a significant provider of funds for social services. As it did so, however, it made specific provision, through the 1962 amendments to the Social Security Act and even more so in the 1967 amendments, for state agencies to enlist nonprofit organizations in the actual delivery of the services.[5] By 1971, in fact, purchases from nonprofit providers constituted about 25 percent of the expenditures under various social service programs that in 1972 were folded into the federal Title XX program, and that ultimately became part of the Social Services Block Grant program in 1981. This pattern of contracting out has, moreover, increased even further in recent years.[6]

---

4. Amos G. Warner, American Charities: A Study in Philanthropy and Economics (New York: Thomas Y. Crowell, 1894), pp. 336-337.

5. Specific provisions for state contracting out to nonprofit organizations were included in the original proposals advanced for federal social service funding by the Kennedy administration in 1962, but the provisions had to be abandoned when religious groups expressed concern about constitutional prohibitions against federal support of religiously affiliated social service agencies. These objections were dropped in 1967 and the provisions added.

6. Bill Benton et al., Social Services: Federal Legislation vs. State Implementation (Washington, D.C.: The Urban Institute, October 1978); U.S. Department of Health and Human Services, Social Services U.S.A. (Washington, D.C.: U.S. Government Printing Office, 1981).

Federal support for nonprofit organizations has evolved similarly in other fields as well--in health care, education, research, neighborhood development, and the arts. In some areas, in fact, federal support has led to the creation of whole new classes of nonprofit organizations to provide a range of services that existing institutions were not equipped to handle and that the federal government did not want to handle on its own. In this way, the federal government has significantly extended the structure of the nonprofit sector. Typical of these developments was the stimulus the federal government gave to the creation of a network of community health clinics in poverty areas throughout the country. Funded originally out of resources provided under the Economic Opportunity Act of 1964, almost 900 such centers existed as of 1980. Other examples of the same kind include the creation of a network of multicounty economic development districts to stimulate economic development in distressed areas, the formation of community action agencies and Head Start programs for disadvantaged children, and the organization of metropolitan councils of government (COGs) to encourage regional planning in metropolitan areas.

Scope

Through these and other channels, an elaborate system of federal support for nonprofit organizations has taken shape in this country. Broadly speaking, this support flows along three main routes, though it takes a variety of different forms. As reflected in figure 5, one of these routes involves direct financial relationships between the federal

Figure 5
Channels of Public Funding of Nonprofit Organizations

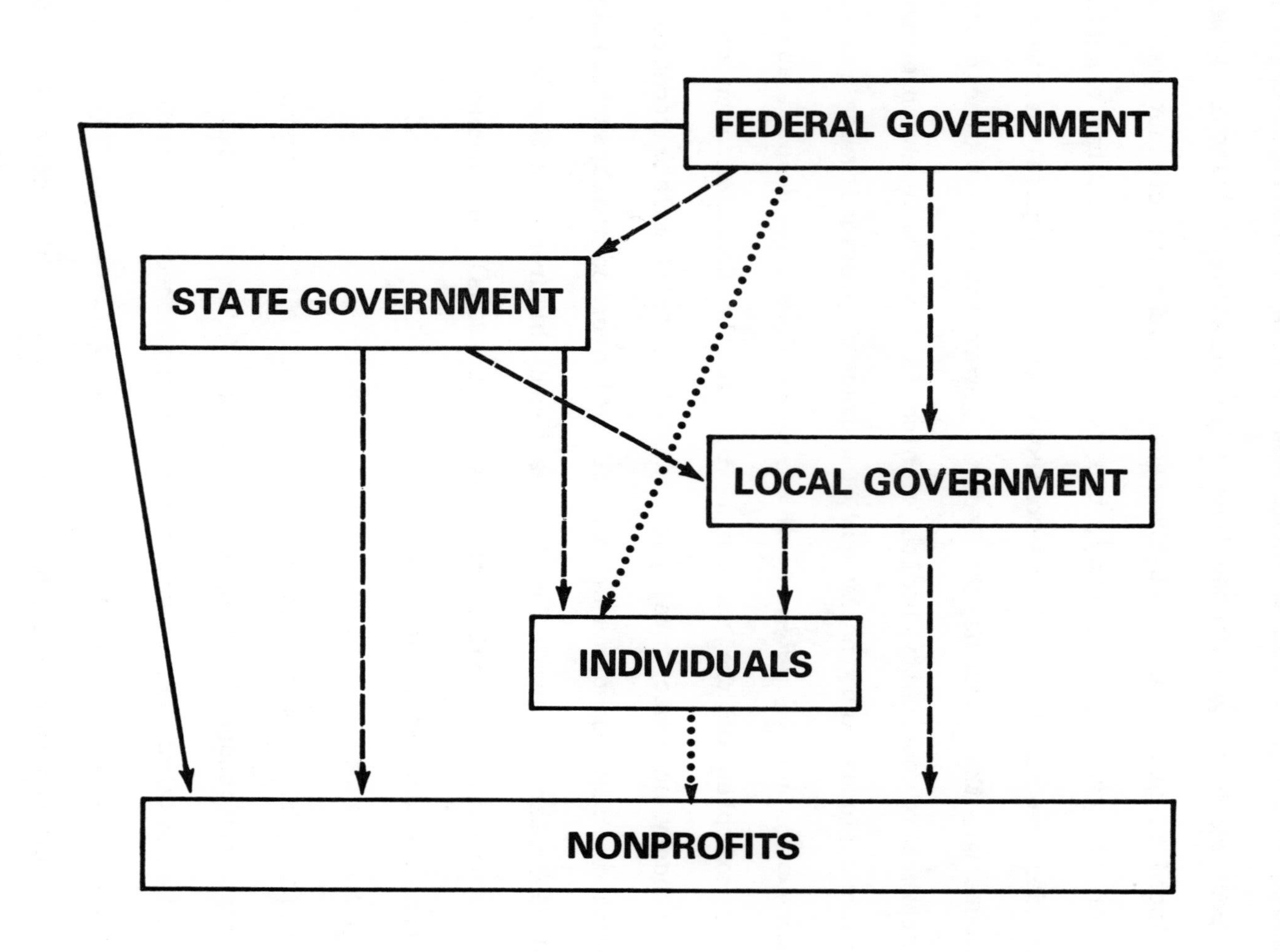

government and nonprofit organizations. An example would be a federal research grant to a private medical school. The second route involves federal grants to state and local governments, which then contract out to nonprofit providers or others to deliver a particular service. A classic example here is the Social Service Block Grant program, which channels federal assistance to the states and leaves to the states the option of providing the services themselves, contracting with other levels of government, or contracting with for-profit or nonprofit providers. Finally, the third route involves federal in-kind assistance to individuals, who then are free to purchase services from nonprofit institutions. This is the route followed in the college student assistance programs and in Medicare.

Despite the scale and importance of this system of support, no comprehensive statistical data are assembled on it anywhere in the federal government. There is no data source on federal support to nonprofits that is comparable, for example, to the special analysis prepared by the Office of Management and Budget each year on the extent of federal grant-in-aid support to state and local governments and the way this will be affected by proposed budget changes. Nor does reliable information exist on funds channeled to nonprofits by individual programs. As a consequence, policymakers and nonprofit managers have had to operate very much in the dark with respect to the effects of budget decisions on this important sector of national life.

To remedy this situation, we developed estimates of the share of program resources flowing to nonprofit organizations under each of the federal programs identified above as being relevant to the nonprofit sector. These estimates were based on detailed examination of programmatic data, scrutiny of existing program evaluations, and extensive discussions with program managers.[7]

Drawing on this analysis, we found that in FY 1980 federal support to the nonprofit sector, exclusive of tax subsidies, amounted to more than $40 billion, as noted in figure 6. Given the size of the sector discussed earlier, this means that the federal government accounts for about 35 percent of the sector's total revenues. By comparison, as we have seen, private charitable contributions to nonprofit service providers from individuals, corporations, and foundations combined totaled $26.8 billion that same year. In other words, nonprofit organizations other than churches now derive a larger share of their revenues from the federal government than from all of private giving combined.[8]

---

7. For a more detailed discussion of the estimating procedure, see Lester M. Salamon with Alan J. Abramson, The Federal Government and the Nonprofit Sector: Implications of the Reagan Budget Proposals (Washington, D.C.: The Urban Institute, May 1981), pp. 35-38. Included in the figures on federal support to nonprofits is the federal subsidy to nonprofits through reduced mail rates. The total federal mail rate subsidy has been apportioned among the various types of nonprofit organizations according to estimates based in part on U.S. Postal Service studies.

8. This finding is consistent with the estimates developed by the Commission on Private Philanthropy and Public Needs (the Filer Commission) in 1974. According to these estimates, all public support to the nonprofit sector (including state and local as well as federal government support) totaled $23.1 billion in 1974, compared with a total of $13.6 billion in private giving to nonprofits excluding churches and other religious organizations. See Gabriel Rudney, "The Scope of the Private Voluntary Charitable Sector," Research Papers Sponsored by the Commission on Private Philanthropy and Public Needs (Washington, D.C.: U.S. Department of the Treasury, 1977), pp. 135-42.

Figure 6
Nonprofit Revenues From Federal Sources, FY 1980
($ Billions)

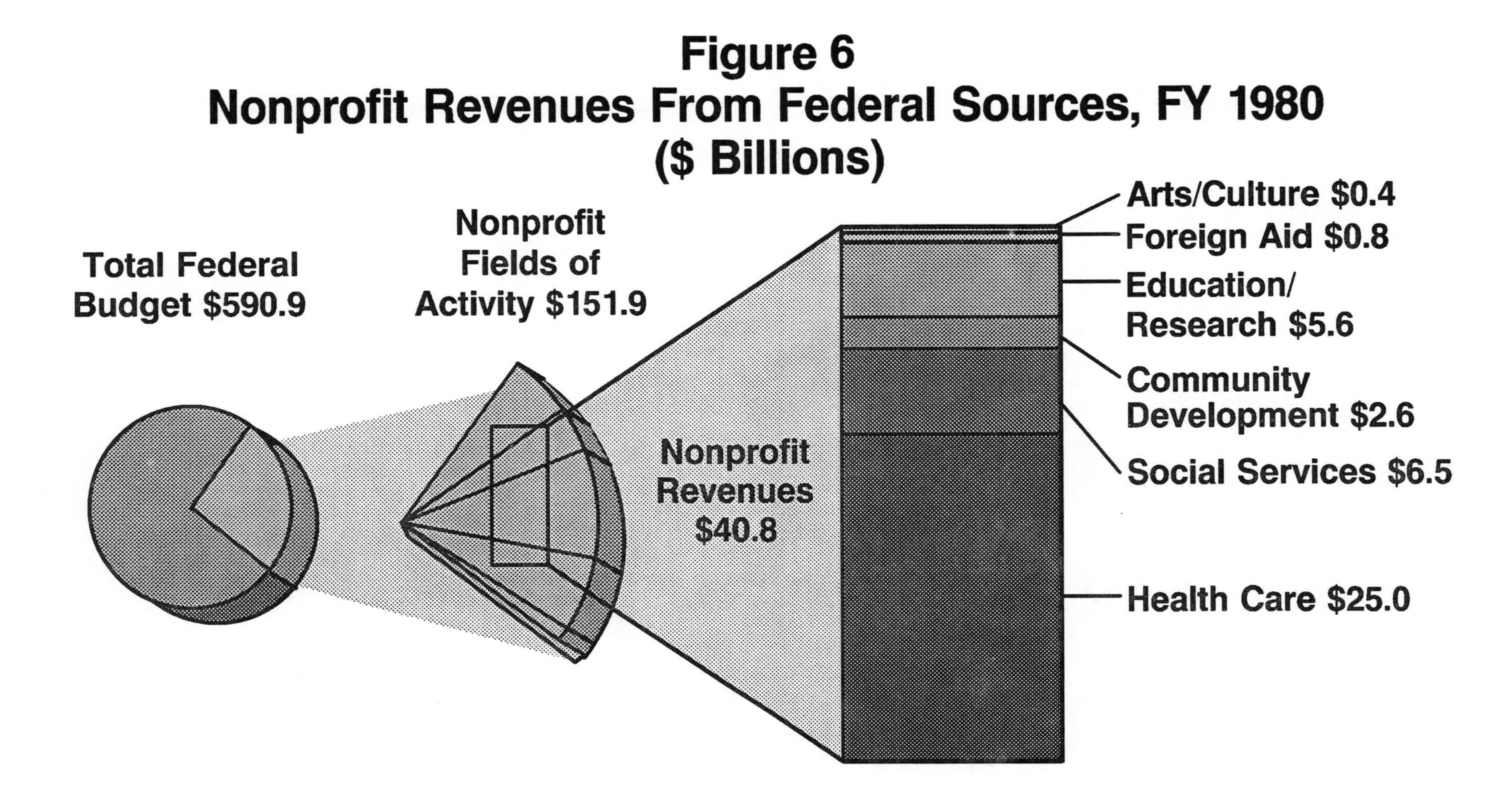

Source: The Urban Institute Nonprofit Sector Project, Based on the Application of the Authors' Nonprofit Share Estimates to Actual FY 1980 Outlay Data in OMB, Budget, FY 1982, Unpublished Backup Material

As figure 6 shows, more than 60 percent of this federal support to nonprofit organizations flows to health care organizations, mostly hospitals. This reflects the tremendous scale of the federal Medicare program, which reimburses hospitals for medical care to the elderly; and the Medicaid program, which underwrites hospital and nursing home care for the elderly poor. In addition, however, social service and education and research institutions also receive substantial amounts of federal support. In fact, as shown in table 9, nonprofit social service organizations received over half their total revenues from federal sources in FY 1980. Other types of nonprofit organizations were somewhat less dependent on federal sources of support, but for virtually all types, this support is a significant component of overall revenues, typically outdistancing private giving by a substantial margin.[9] Under these circumstances, nonprofit organizations have far more than a casual stake in federal budget decisions. These decisions are now one of the major determinants of the fiscal health of the sector, and of the viability of several of its components.

---

9. Private giving appears to outdistance federal support only for educational and cultural organizations, but in both these cases the private giving figure is swelled by the inclusion of the full value of bequests and appreciated assets in the year in which they are given even though they are not available for use.

Table 9

Nonprofit Revenues from Federal Sources
Compared to Private Giving and Total Nonprofit Revenues,
by Type of Organization, FY 1980
(Billions of Dollars unless Otherwise Indicated)

Type of Organization	Total Revenue	Private Giving	Federal Programs	Federal Support as a Percent of Total Revenue
Social Service[a]	$ 13.2[a]	$ 5.0	$ 7.3[a]	55%
Community Development, Civic	5.4	1.5	2.6	48
Education/Research	25.2	6.9	5.6	22
Health Care	70.0	6.7	25.0	36
Arts/Culture	2.6	3.2[b]	0.4	15
Other	--	3.5	--	--
Total	$116.4	$26.8	$40.8	35

SOURCE: The Urban Institute Nonprofit Sector Project, see table 2.

a. Includes social services and foreign aid.

b. Includes endowment revenue and contributions of appreciated assets such as works of art.

In short, an immense and complex set of partnership arrangements has developed between the federal government and nonprofit organizations. These arrangements have deep roots in American history. Most of them operate indirectly, through state and local governments and individual purchasers of services. Taken together, however, they account for a substantial share of nonprofit revenues, especially for social service and community development organizations. Indeed, in dollar terms, they represent a larger share of nonprofit revenues than all of private giving combined. While the relationships that lie behind these figures have not been without their strains, they also have had much to recommend them. They have offered an innovative way to combine the revenue-raising advantages of the federal government with the service-providing advantages of private, voluntary agencies. As such, they represent an important adaptation in the design of the modern welfare state.

The Impact of Enacted Budget Changes on Nonprofit Revenues

The budget and program changes enacted in the first five fiscal years of the Reagan presidency, FY 1982-86, have posed a significant challenge to this set of partnership arrangements. The spending reductions discussed in chapter 3 have already cut significantly into federal support for nonprofit organizations in a number of areas. As figure 7 demonstrates, while growth in the federal Medicare and Medicaid programs boosted the value of federal support to private, nonprofit health institutions--principally hospitals--federal support for most other types of nonprofit organizations fell sharply between FY 1981 and FY 1982 and then remained at this reduced level through FY 1986. As reflected in the bottom part of table 10, the inflation-adjusted value of federal support of nonprofits through programs other than Medicare and Medicaid

Figure 7
Changes in Federal Support of Nonprofits*

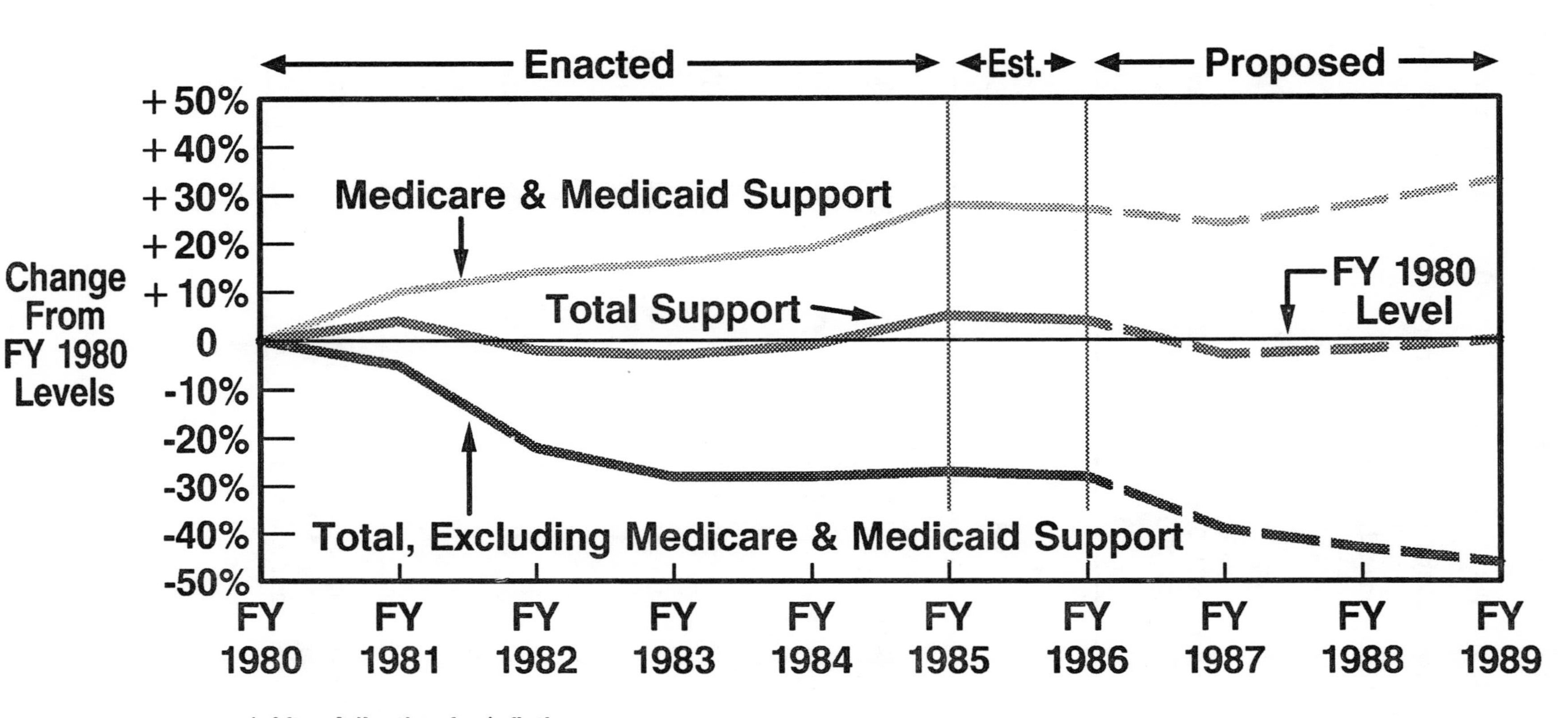

* After Adjusting for Inflation

Source: The Urban Institute Nonprofit Sector Project, Adapted From OMB, Budget, FY 1987 and Preceding Years After Application of Authors' Nonprofit Sahre Estimates

thus declined by a total of $23.0 billion over this five-year period, or about $4.6 billion per year below what would have been available had FY 1980 levels been maintained. This represents a 27 percent decline in the value of this federal support.

Table 10

Enacted Year-to-Year Changes in
Federal Support of Nonprofit Organizations, FY 1980-86, in Constant FY 1980 Dollars
(Billions of Dollars unless Otherwise Indicated)

Type of Support	FY 1980	FY 1981	FY 1982	FY 1983	FY 1984	FY 1985	FY 1986	Total, FY 1982-86
All Federal Support								
Amount	$40.8	$42.3	$40.2	$39.8	$40.5	$42.8	$42.3	$205.5
Change from FY 1980								
Amount		+$1.5	-$0.7	-$1.0	-$0.4	+$1.9	+$1.5	+$1.4
Percentage		+4%	-2%	-3%	-1%	+5%	+4%	+1%
Medicare, Medicaid								
Amount	$23.5	$25.9	$26.7	$27.3	$28.1	$30.1	$29.8	$142.1
Change from FY 1980								
Amount		+$2.3	+$3.2	+$3.8	+$4.5	+$6.6	+$6.3	+$24.3
Percentage		+10%	+14%	+16%	+19%	+28%	+27%	+21%
Total, without Medicare, Medicaid								
Amount	$17.3	$16.5	$13.4	$12.5	$12.4	$12.6	$12.5	$63.4
Change from FY 1980								
Amount		-$0.8	-$3.9	-$4.8	-$4.9	-$4.7	-$4.8	-$23.0
Percentage		-5%	-22%	-28%	-28%	-27%	-28%	-27%

SOURCE: The Urban Institute Nonprofit Sector Project, based on data in OMB, Budget, FY 1987 and preceding years, unpublished backup material, after application of nonprofit share estimates developed in Salamon and Abramson, The Federal Budget and the Nonprofit Sector.

Table 11

Enacted Changes in Federal Support of Nonprofit Organizations,
by Type of Organization, FY 1982-86 versus FY 1980,
in Constant FY 1980 Dollars
(Billions of Dollars unless Otherwise Indicated)

Type of Organization	FY 1980	Changes From FY 1980 Levels: Actual FY 1982	Actual FY 1983	Actual FY 1984	Actual FY 1985	Estimated FY 1986	Total, FY 1982-86	Percent Change, FY 1986 vs. FY 1980
Social Service	$ 6.5	-$2.1	-$2.5	-$2.4	-$2.5	-$2.6	-$12.0	-40%
Community Development	2.6	-0.6	-0.7	-0.9	-1.0	-1.1	-4.4	-44
Education/Research	5.6	-0.5	-0.8	-0.8	-0.6	-0.4	-3.1	-7
Elementary/Secondary	0.4	-0.2	-0.2	-0.2	-0.2	-0.2	-1.1	-60
Higher Education	2.7	-0.3	-0.4	-0.7	-0.6	-0.6	-2.6	-21
Research/Development	2.6	0.0	-0.1	+0.1	+0.2	+0.4	+0.6	+16
Health Care	25.0	+2.9	+3.3	+4.0	+6.1	+5.8	+22.1	+23
Health Finance	23.6	+3.2	+3.7	+4.5	+6.6	+6.3	+24.3	+27
Health Services	1.4	-0.2	-0.5	-0.4	-0.5	-0.5	-2.1	-37
Foreign Aid	0.8	-0.2	-0.2	-0.1	0.0	-0.1	-0.5	-8
Arts/Culture	0.4	-0.1	-0.2	-0.2	-0.2	-0.2	-0.8	-41
Total	$40.8	-$0.7	-$1.0	-$0.4	+$1.9	+$1.5	+$1.4	+4
Total, excluding Medicare, Medicaid	$17.3	-$3.9	-$4.8	-$4.9	-$4.7	-$4.8	-$23.0	-28

SOURCE: The Urban Institute Nonprofit Sector Project, see table 10.

In some fields, moreover, the reductions were even more severe than this. Thus social service, community development, and arts and humanities organizations lost about 40 percent of their federal support while significant losses were also registered by health clinics and higher education institutions. Table 11 summarizes some of the major changes by type of agency. What lies behind this table are the following kinds of changes:

Social service organizations. Social service organizations--including agencies that provide day-care, counseling, and related services to children, families, the elderly, and others; legal services; and employment and training services--were the biggest losers of government support over the FY 1982-86 period. These agencies lost a total of $12.0 billion in federal support during this five-year period, or about $2.4 billion a year. By FY 1986, therefore, the income they received through federal programs was projected to be 40 percent below what it had been in FY 1980.

These losses resulted from significant spending reductions in youth training, public service employment, community services, Social Services Block Grant, and legal services programs, all of which made heavy use of nonprofit providers. Compared to FY 1985 levels, the changes projected for FY 1986, including the initial Gramm-Rudman-Hollings cuts, account for reductions to nonprofit social service agencies of about 3 percent.

Community development organizations. Organizations involved in housing, housing rehabilitation, economic development, and neighborhood improvement suffered the second largest reductions in federal support over FY 1982-86, with cumulative losses of $4.4 billion below FY 1980 levels. This includes a 6 percent reduction in FY 1986 below the already-reduced FY 1985 level. By FY 1986, federal support to community development organizations is therefore projected to be 44 percent below what it was in FY 1980. These cuts reflect changes that eliminated or sharply curtailed several programs specifically designed to encourage nonprofit involvement in this field, including the community economic development program, housing for the elderly or handicapped, and the neighborhood self-help development program.

Education/research. For education and research organizations, two competing pressures were at work. On the one hand, federal support for education activities declined between FY 1980 and FY 1986--by 21 percent for higher education and by 60 percent for the more limited elementary and secondary education support. On the other hand, federal research and development support for private nonprofit institutions increased, reaching 16 percent above its FY 1980 level by FY 1986. This largely reflected the growth of defense-related scientific research.

Because many higher education institutions are affected by both the education and research support, they may have cancelled some of their education losses through research gains. It is important to note, however, that the net reduction of $3.1 billion, or 7 percent, in the value of federal support to nonprofit education and research organizations really disguised a cumulative decline of $3.6 billion in the value of federal educational support coupled with an $0.6 billion gain in research.

Health organizations. Even nonprofit health organizations were not immune from cuts. While federal support for nonprofit hospitals, nursing homes, and other providers through the Medicare and, to a lesser extent, Medicaid programs increased, support for outpatient clinics and other health service organizations declined. By FY 1985, such support had already fallen by 33 percent below its FY 1980 level. Between FY 1985 and FY 1986, it is projected to fall another 5 percent. As a result, by the end of FY 1986, such support is projected to be 37 percent lower than it was in FY 1980.

Foreign aid organizations. Although overall federal foreign assistance outlays went up over FY 1982-86, as described in chapter 3, federal support to nonprofits in this program area--including American-based nonprofits providing nutrition assistance, health care, education assistance, and other services abroad--registered a decline of $0.5 billion. This decline resulted from reductions in funding of programs that rely to some extent on nonprofits to deliver services, such as the Public Law 480 food assistance and refugee assistance programs. Between FY 1985 and FY 1986 alone, this support is estimated to decline by 13 percent.

Arts and culture organizations. Federal support to nonprofit arts and cultural agencies, such as museums, art galleries, symphonies, community arts facilities, and theaters, is projected to be 41 percent lower in FY 1986 than it was in FY 1980. A significant portion of this loss resulted from the elimination of the public service employment program which provided important support to numerous community arts agencies; but estimated inflation-adjusted losses of 17 to 36 percent were also registered in nonprofit receipts from the National Endowment for the Arts, the National Endowment for the Humanities, and the Corporation for Public Broadcasting.

Summary. Outside of the health finance area, the federal government pulled back significantly from its partnership arrangements with private, nonprofit organizations during the five years ending in FY 1986. Compared to what they received in FY 1980 outside of Medicare and Medicaid support, nonprofit organizations lost 27 percent of their federal support as of FY 1985 and this will sink to 28 percent by the end of FY 1986. While the total level of federal support to nonprofit organizations held relatively constant during this period, the share absorbed by hospitals and other recipients of Medicare and Medicaid climbed from 58 percent in FY 1980 to 71 percent in FY 1986, and the share left for all other types of nonprofit organizations declined from 42 percent to 29 percent. In short, while being called on to do more, these organizations lost a significant share of the revenues they needed just to stay where they were.

The New Reagan Budget and Nonprofit Revenues

These nonprofit losses would be further intensified by the new budget proposed by the Reagan administration for the period FY 1987 to FY 1989, as shown by the dotted lines in figure 7. In particular, for FY 1987 these proposals would reduce federal support to nonprofit organizations--outside of Medicare and Medicaid recipients--by 17 percent below the already-reduced 1985 levels, and these reductions would deepen over the subsequent two years. As shown in table 12, these nonprofit organizations would therefore receive a total of $22.2 billion less in federal support over these three years than if FY 1980 levels had been maintained. This represents losses of about $7.4 billion a year over this three-year period, compared to the $4.6 billion-a-year reductions sustained over the previous five years. By FY 1989, federal support to nonprofits in these fields would thus be cut almost in half (46 percent) compared to what it was in FY 1980.

Table 12

Proposed Year-to-Year Changes in Federal Support of Nonprofit Organizations, FY 1980, FY 1987-89 versus FY 1980, in Constant FY 1980 Dollars
(Billions of Dollars unless Otherwise Indicated)

Type of Support	FY 1980	FY 1987	FY 1988	FY 1989	Total FY 1987-89
All Federal Support					
Amount	$40.8	$39.8	$39.9	$40.6	$120.3
Change from FY 1980					
Amount		-$1.0	-$1.0	-$0.2	-$2.2
Percentage		-3%	-2%	0%	-2%
Medicare, Medicaid					
Amount	$23.5	$29.3	$30.1	$31.3	$ 90.7
Change from FY 1980					
Amount		+$5.7	+$6.5	+$7.8	+$20.0
Percentage		+24%	+28%	+33%	+28%
Total, without Medicare, Medicaid					
Amount	$17.3	$10.5	$ 9.8	$ 9.3	$ 29.6
Change from FY 1980					
Amount		-$6.7	-$7.5	-$7.9	-$22.2
Percentage		-39%	-43%	-46%	-43%

SOURCE: The Urban Institute Nonprofit Sector Project, see table 10.

As before, social service and community development organizations absorb the bulk of these cuts as shown in table 13 and figure 8. Thus, if the president's budget were enacted, by FY 1989 the value of federal support to nonprofit social service organizations would be 55 percent below what it was in FY 1980, and for community development organizations it would be 71 percent lower. But substantial reductions below FY 1980 levels would also be in store for private higher education institutions (down 55 percent), health service organizations (down 47 percent), and arts and humanities institutions (down 62 percent). The proposed termination of the Treasury reimbursement to the Postal Service for subsidized mail rates for nonprofits would also reduce federal support to a wide range of nonprofits.[10] The discussion below summarizes the proposed changes that account for these reductions:

Social service organizations. Under the president's new budget, in FY 1987 nonprofit social service organizations would receive 20 percent less federal support than they received last year in FY 1985, which was already 38 percent below the level that existed in FY 1980. For the entire FY 1987-89 period, social service organizations would lose a total of $10.4 billion in federal support compared to what they would have received if FY 1980 levels had persisted, a reduction of about $3.5 billion a year, compared to the losses of $2.4 billion a year over the

---

10. The president's FY 1987 budget states that legislation will be proposed to allow the Postal Service to continue the nonprofit mail rate subsidy on its own. However, no federal money is earmarked for this purpose in the budget. For the purposes of this report, therefore, it was assumed that the subsidy will terminate in FY 1986.

prior five years. By FY 1989, therefore, these organizations would receive about 55 percent less in federal aid than they got in FY 1980. Planned reductions in youth training programs and the proposed elimination of the community services and legal services programs, which rely heavily on nonprofits to deliver services, account for the largest portion of these losses to nonprofits.

Table 13

Proposed Changes in Federal Support of Nonprofits, by Type of Organization, FY 1987-89, in Constant FY 1980 Dollars (Billions of Dollars)

		Changes from FY 1980 Levels					
		Actual	Proposed				Percent Change,
Type of Organization	FY 1980	FY 1985	FY 1987	FY 1988	FY 1989	Total FY 1987-89	FY 1989 versus FY 1980
Social Service	$ 6.5	-$2.5	-$3.3	-$3.5	-$3.6	-$10.4	-55
Community Development	2.6	-1.0	-1.5	-1.7	-1.8	-5.0	-71
Education/Research	5.6	-0.6	-1.0	-1.3	-1.4	-3.7	-25
Elementary/Secondary	0.4	-0.2	-0.3	-0.3	-0.3	-0.8	-71
Higher Education	2.7	-0.6	-1.1	-1.5	-1.5	-4.0	-55
Research/Development	2.6	+0.2	+0.4	+0.4	+0.3	+1.1	+12
Health Care	25.0	+6.1	+5.0	+5.9	+7.1	+18.0	+28
Health Finance	23.6	+6.6	+5.7	+6.5	+7.7	+19.9	+33
Health Services	1.4	-0.5	-0.6	-0.6	-0.7	-1.9	-47
Foreign Aid	0.8	0.0	-0.1	-0.2	-0.2	-0.5	-22
Arts/Culture	0.4	-0.2	-0.2	-0.2	-0.2	-0.6	-62
Total	$40.8	+$1.9	-$1.0	-$1.0	-$0.2	-$2.2	0
Total, excluding Medicare, Medicaid	$17.3	-$4.7	-$6.7	-$7.5	-$7.9	-$22.2	-46

SOURCE: The Urban Institute Nonprofit Sector Project, see table 10.

Figure 8
Changes in Nonprofit Revenues From Federal Sources, FY 1989 and FY 1985 Vs. FY 1980*

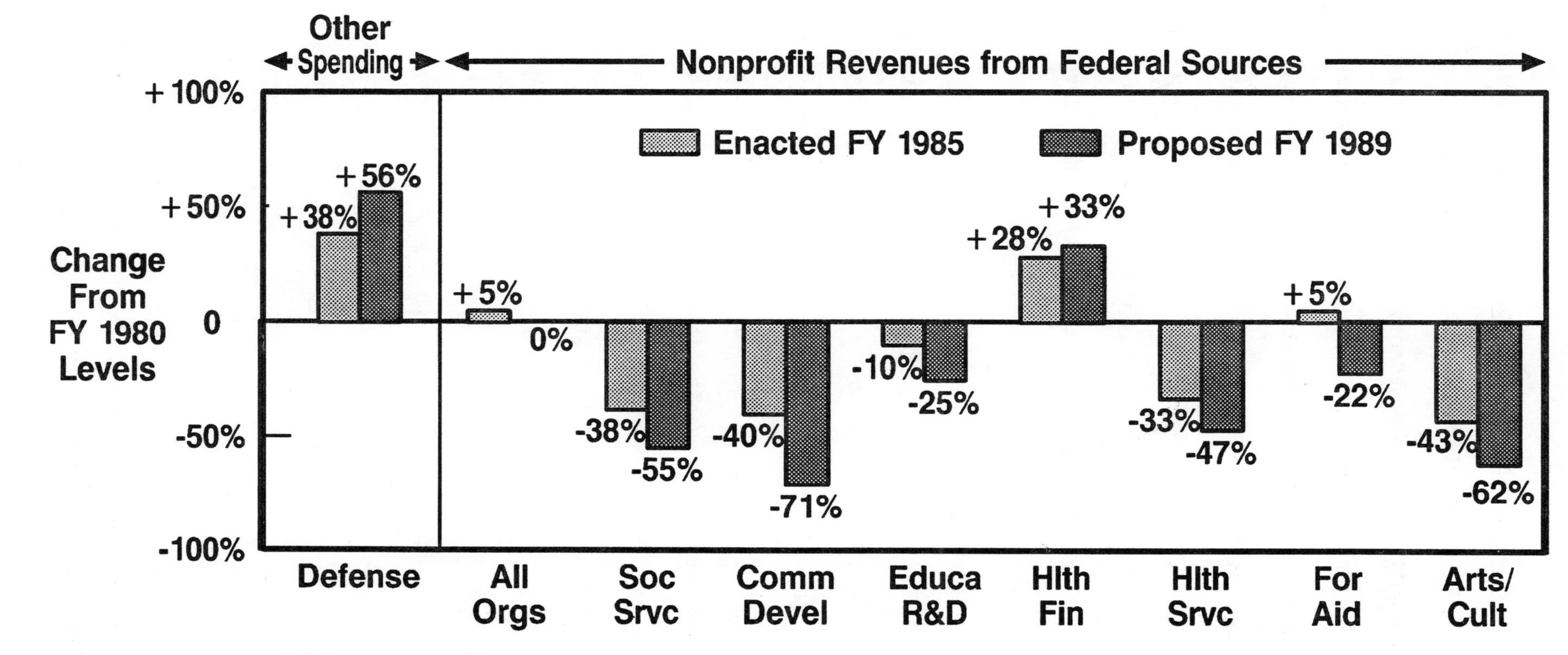

* Adjusted for Inflation

Source: The Urban Institute Nonprofit Sector Project, Adapted From OMB, Budget, FY 1987 Based on Application of the Authors' Nonprofit Share Estimates

Community development organizations. Community development organizations would be particularly hard hit by proposals in the new budget to allow no new activity in the elderly and handicapped housing program, to eliminate the emergency food and shelter program and historic preservation fund, and to cut back drastically the energy conservation grant program. As a result of these and other new reductions, federal support to nonprofit community development organizations in FY 1987 would drop an additional 29 percent below already-reduced FY 1985 levels. Coupled with the reductions previously enacted, community development organizations would thus lose $5.0 billion in federal support over FY 1987-89 compared to what they would have received had FY 1980 levels persisted. By FY 1989, federal support to these organizations would thus be 71 percent below what it was in FY 1980. In this field, therefore, the federal partnership with the nonprofit sector would be all but be eliminated.

Education/research organizations. Among education and research organizations, private, nonprofit colleges and universities would lose federal support as the result of proposed reductions in the student loan guarantee, Pell Grant, and other student financial assistance programs. Between FY 1985 and FY 1987, federal support to nonprofit higher education institutions would thus sink another 23 percent. By FY 1989 it would be 55 percent below what it was in FY 1980. Nonprofit research organizations involved in many areas of domestic policy research would lose support, but gains by those involved in defense and National Science Foundation research would more than offset this, so that overall research support to private nonprofit organizations would grow by 12 percent by FY 1989.

Health organizations. As a whole, health organizations would receive $18.0 billion more under the president's new budget than they would have received had FY 1980 levels persisted, as shown in table 13. However, this is largely a result of increased Medicare spending. By contrast, support to nonprofit health service organizations and clinics outside the Medicare and Medicaid system would be reduced sharply. Such support would decline by 16 percent between FY 1985 and FY 1987 alone. As a result of these and subsequent cuts these organizations would end up with about 47 percent less in federal support in FY 1989 than they received in FY 1980. The principal sources of these reductions are further cuts proposed for the Alcohol, Drug Abuse, and Mental Health Block Grant, the Primary Care Block Grant, and Health Resources and Services Administration programs. Moreover, while federal support to health care providers through Medicare and Medicaid will remain well above its FY 1980 level, the administration proposes to restrain the growth of these programs by limiting the increases in prospective payments under the new diagnosis-related groups (DRG) payment system, by eliminating separate capital cost payments to hospitals, by increasing cost-sharing, and through other means. In the Medicaid program, in fact, the increases over FY 1980 levels are misleading since FY 1981 levels were actually higher than FY 1980, and significant reductions have occurred from these FY 1981 levels.

Foreign aid organizations. Further real reductions in spending in the Public Law 480 food assistance and refugee assistance programs would also cut into federal support for nonprofit organizations involved in international relief. Between FY 1985 and FY 1987, such support would fall by over 20 percent. As a result, these organizations will end up by FY 1989 with 22 percent less federal support than they had in FY 1980.

Arts organizations. Federal support for nonprofit arts organizations would drop each year from FY 1987 to FY 1989 under the president's proposed budget as a result of reductions in a number of programs, including the proposed elimination of the Institute of Museum Services and the Treasury subsidy of nonprofit mail rates. Arts organizations are projected by FY 1989 to have 62 percent less federal support than they had in FY 1980.

Summary

In short, the Reagan administration's FY 1987 budget would further reduce the value of federal support to nonprofit organizations outside of Medicare and Medicaid. Coupled with the reductions already put into effect over the previous five years, these cuts would severely undercut the partnership arrangements between government and the voluntary sector that had formed over the preceding decades, especially in the fields of social services, community development, higher education, and arts and culture. Federal support in many of these fields would be cut nearly in half or more, further limiting the ability of these organizations to maintain prior service levels let alone to expand to meet new needs left behind by overall government withdrawal.

How significant a problem this creates for these agencies, however, depends not only on the extent of their governmental losses, but also on the availability of alternative revenues to fill the resulting gap. Of particular importance, moreover, is the availability of private charitable support, since it is the shifting from government to private support that is a principal objective of the budgetary changes that are being proposed. It is therefore necessary to inquire whether private charitable support was able to fill in for the overall cutbacks in federal spending that have already occurred; and, if not, whether private charitable support was at least able to offset the direct revenue losses that nonprofit agencies sustained during this period. We can then assess the increases in private giving that would be needed to offset the additional cuts in these programs proposed over the next three years. It is to these tasks that we turn in the next chapter.

CHAPTER 5

THE CHALLENGE TO PRIVATE GIVING

One of the central questions surrounding the recent round of federal budget cuts has to do not so much with the size of the cuts as with the possibility for offsetting them through private action. This question arises naturally from the line of thinking that views government and charitable institutions as alternative ways of meeting public objectives. As government withdraws, therefore, it is reasonable to ask what portion of the resulting gap can reasonably be filled through private charitable activity, and what level of change in such activity is needed to accomplish this goal.

As reflected in the previous chapters, however, this question really involves two separate issues. As we have seen, federal budget cuts affect not only the need for nonprofit services, but also the revenues available to nonprofits to meet this need. Both of these represent a challenge to private giving and both must therefore be assessed.

It is the purpose of this chapter to provide such an assessment. In particular, this chapter first examines the extent to which private giving has managed to offset the reductions that have already occurred both in overall federal spending in fields where nonprofits are active and in the revenues of nonprofit agencies between FY 1982 and FY 1984, the most recent year for which private giving data are available. It then projects the rate of increase in private giving required to offset these same two budget-related impacts on nonprofits resulting from the budget changes already enacted for FY 1985 and FY 1986 as well as those proposed in the president's budget for FY 1987-89.

In making this comparison, it is not our intention to suggest that everything the federal government has supported is worthy of continued support by the private sector or anyone else, or that private charity should be used for the same things as government funds. Nor is there any suggestion here that private support is in some sense "better" than public support, or vice versa. Rather, it is our intent to put the cuts that have occurred or are being proposed into some perspective and to shed some solid, factual light on a comparison that has too often been a subject of much too casual speculation.

Has Private Giving Offset the Budget Cuts to Date?

The Charitable Base

In FY 1980, the year before Mr. Reagan took office, private giving from all sources totaled about $47.73 billion.[1] This is a somewhat generous estimate, however, since it includes bequests, endowment giving, and gifts of appreciated assets (such as works of art) that are not really available to defray the costs of service provision in the year in which the gift is given.

Of this $47.73 billion in private giving, about $26.78 billion went to churches and synagogues for sacramental religious activities or to

---

1. The fiscal year figures for private giving reported here are adapted from calendar year data in Giving USA: 1985 Annual Report (New York: American Association of Fund-Raising Counsel, 1985). Fiscal year data are used to make the private giving figures comparable to the federal budget figures. Note that the calendar year private giving figures were reported in chapters 2 and 4.

health organizations which did not experience reductions in either the overall level of federal activity or in their levels of federal support. This leaves about $20.95 billion in private giving as of FY 1980 for the types of organizations that were negatively affected by the federal budget cuts of the early 1980s.[2]

Private Giving and The Service Gap

As we have seen, federal spending in fields where nonprofits are active, excluding health, declined significantly in the early 1980s. As shown in column 1 of Table 5-1, between FY 1982 and FY 1984, the latest year for which private giving data are available, overall federal spending in these fields dropped a total of $41.81 billion below what it would have been had FY 1980 spending levels been maintained.

Compared to this $41.81 billion cut in federal support, private giving for other than sacramental religious purposes and health increased by only $3.10 billion during this same period after adjusting for inflation, as shown in column 3 of this same table. In other words, the growth in private giving during these three years offset only 7 percent of the reduction in government spending that occurred.

To be sure, private giving made up a larger share of the cuts in FY 1984, which was a peak growth year for private giving, than in the other years. But even in FY 1984 private giving was only able to compensate

2. Sacramental religious activities are estimated to absorb about 93 percent of the private giving to religious organizations which is reported in Giving USA. This estimate of the amount of religious giving which goes for sacramental religious purposes is based on research summarized in Lester M. Salamon and Fred Teitelbaum, "Religious Congregations As Social Service Agencies: How Extensive Are They?" Foundation News, vol. 25, no. 5 (September/October 1984), pp. 62-65.

for 16 percent of the federal cutbacks in these fields. If nonprofit organizations filled a significant share of the gap in service provision created by government spending cuts, therefore, they did not do so through private, charitable support.

Table 14

Changes in Federal Spending and Private Charitable Support in Fields of Interest to Nonprofit Organizations, in Constant FY 1980 Dollars
(Billions of Dollars unless Otherwise Indicated)

	Change From FY 1980 Level			Private Giving Change as Percentage	
Fiscal Year	Federal Spending in Areas of Interest to Nonprofits[a]	Federal Support of Nonprofits[a]	Private Giving[b]	Change in Federal Spending in Areas of Interest To Nonprofits	Change in Federal Support of Nonprofits
1982	-$12.88	-$ 3.59	-$0.29	-2%	-8%
1983	-13.71	-4.33	+0.89	+6	+21
1984	-15.22	-4.40	+2.50	+16	+57
Total	-$41.81	-$12.32	+$3.10	+7	+25

SOURCE: Figures for private giving are adapted from calendar year (CY) data in Giving USA: 1985 Annual Report (New York: American Association of Fund-Raising Counsel, 1985). Calculations are by The Urban Institute Nonprofit Sector Project.

a. Excludes Medicare, Medicaid, and all other health programs.

b. Private giving to other than health or sacramental religious organizations; includes 7 percent of religious giving; excludes a one-time gift to the arts of $1.3 billion in CY 1982.

Private Giving and Past Changes in Nonprofit Revenues

Not only was private giving unable to offset the overall reductions in federal spending in fields where nonprofit organizations are active, however. It also was unable to offset the direct revenue losses that nonprofits experienced as a consequence.

As shown in column 2 of table 14, these revenue losses totaled $12.32 billion during the three years FY 1982-84. The $3.10 billion in real growth in private giving that occurred in these fields during this same period therefore made up for at most 25 percent of the revenue losses nonprofits experienced.

Here as well, the FY 1984 experience was far better than average. But even in this year, private giving made up only 57 percent of the reductions in revenues that nonprofit agencies experienced as a result of the federal budget cuts. In short, far from providing the support needed to enable nonprofits to expand their activities to fill the gap left by federal reductions, the growth in private giving was not even sufficient to allow nonprofits to maintain their prior activity levels.[3]

Can Private Giving Offset the Proposed Budget Cuts?

Although private giving has not managed to offset the reductions that occurred either in overall federal spending in fields where nonpro-

---

3. Other work we have done on nonprofit sector finances suggests that the nonprofit sector did manage to maintain its overall spending level during this period, but mostly by increasing its fees and service charges, not by raising sufficient private charitable support. See: Lester M. Salamon, "Nonprofits: The Results Are Coming In," Foundation News, vol. 25, no. 4 (July/August 1984), pp. 16-23.

fits are active or in nonprofit receipts from the federal government between FY 1982 and FY 1984, to what extent does the improved performance of private giving in FY 1984 provide a basis for greater confidence in the future?

To answer this question, we projected private giving for nonsacramental religious and nonhealth purposes through the period FY 1985-89 using the most generous assumption possible--namely, that private giving each year would grow at a rate equivalent to the high rate it achieved in FY 1984 (11.6 percent). We then calculated the rate of increase in private giving that would be needed in each year over the prior year to offset the effects of both inflation and the government budget cuts. Finally, we compared the growth rate that will be needed to what has been achieved recently to calculate the percentage change in the rate of growth in private giving that will be required. Obviously, if private giving in practice grows at a rate below 11.6 percent, the figures here will understate the additional increases required, and vice versa.[4]

Private Giving and the Projected Service Gap

Table 15 provides the first part of the answer to this question, focusing on the growth in private giving needed to offset the overall reductions in federal spending in fields where nonprofits are active.

---

4. Based on preliminary data, it appears as of this writing that the growth rate in private giving for 1985 will be in the neighborhood of 9.5 percent, rather than the 11.6 percent assumed here. This means that the additional growth required to offset the cuts will be greater than reported here.

As column 3 of this table shows, the federal budget cuts already enacted in these fields, expressed in "current" dollars, unadjusted for inflation, total about $15 billion and $17 billion in FY 1985 and FY 1986, respectively. To offset these cuts, private giving would have to grow by about 55 percent a year, over 400 percent greater than its recent peak growth rate of 11.6 percent.

Table 15

Change in Private Giving Needed to Offset
Projected Federal Budget Cuts in
Fields of Interest to Nonprofit Organizations, in Current Dollars
(Billions of Dollars unless Otherwise Indicated)

Fiscal Year	Private Giving in Prior Year[a]	Inflation Rate[b]	Estimated Cuts[c]	Percent Change in Private Giving Needed to Offset Budget Cuts and Inflation	Percent Change Needed in Rate of Private Giving Growth
1985	$29.99	3.6%	-$15.05	+53.8%	+464%
1986	33.47	3.4	-17.44	+55.5	+478
1987	37.35	4.1	-31.22	+87.7	+756
1988	41.68	3.9	-36.06	+90.4	+779
1989	46.51	3.4	-41.62	+92.9	+801

SOURCE: The Urban Institute Nonprofit Sector Project, see tables 4 and 13.

a. Private giving for other than sacramental religious and health purposes; assumes giving will grow at FY 1984 rate of 11.6 percent.

b. Based on administration fiscal year economic assumptions.

c. Excludes health, and is given in current dollars.

This rate of growth would have to increase further during FY 1987-89, moreover, if the president's new budget proposals were enacted. In particular, to offset the cuts proposed for the next three years, private giving during FY 1987-89 would have to jump about 90 percent--almost 800 percent higher than its recent peak rate.

Private Giving and the Projected Losses in Nonprofit Revenues

If it seems unlikely that private giving can be expected to close the entire service gap left by federal spending reductions in fields where nonprofits are active, can it at least offset the direct revenue losses nonprofit organizations are projected to experience as a result of the president's proposed budget cuts?

The answer to this question is provided in table 16. As this table shows, to offset the revenue losses nonprofits have already experienced

Table 16

Change in Private Giving Needed to Offset the Cuts in Federal Support of Nonprofit Organizations, in Current Dollars (Billions of Dollars unless Otherwise Indicated)

Fiscal Year	Private Giving in Prior Year[a]	Inflation Rate[b]	Projected Revenue Loss[c]	Percent Change in Private Giving Needed to Offset Inflation and Nonprofit Revenue Losses	Percent Change Needed in Rate of Private Giving Growth
1985	$29.99	3.6%	-$5.53	+22.0%	+190%
1986	33.47	3.4	-5.86	+20.9	+180
1987	37.35	4.1	-8.66	+27.3	+235
1988	41.68	3.9	-10.10	+28.1	+242
1989	46.51	3.4	-11.06	+27.2	+234

SOURCES: The Urban Institute Nonprofit Sector Project, see tables 4 and 13.

a. Private giving for other than sacramental religious and health purposes; assumes giving will grow at FY 1984 rate of 11.6 percent.

b. Based on administration fiscal year economic assumptions.

c. Excludes health-related losses; given in current dollars.

in FY 1985 and FY 1986, private giving would have to jump by over 20 percent in either of these years. This is nearly 200 percent higher than the recent peak growth rate. What is more, given the additional cuts proposed in the president's latest budget, the rate of growth required over the FY 1987-89 period is in the neighborhood of 27 to 28 percent a year--240 percent higher than the recent peak rate.

Summary

In short, the assumption that is often made that private giving can compensate for cutbacks in federal spending in fields where nonprofits are active seems highly unlikely to say the least. In fact, it is hard to believe that private giving would be able to offset even the direct revenue losses nonprofits would sustain if the budget cuts now being proposed were enacted. Far from being able to expand their services to fill the service gap left by federal withdrawal, nonprofits very likely would have to cut back their own service activities. At the very least, these organizations are likely to continue to experience considerable financial strain--more intensely in some components of the sector (e.g., social services, community development, and higher education) than in others, but affecting all components to some extent.

Beyond the particulars of specific budget decisions, however, the analysis presented here raises broader questions about the whole pattern of government-nonprofit cooperation that has evolved in this country. Reflecting a set of theories that assume a sharp conflict between government and the nonprofit sector, the policies embodied in the Reagan administration's program set out to help the nonprofit sector by getting government out of its way. In fact, however, the realities of government-nonprofit relationships turn out to be far more complex than these theories assume. As a result, a set of policies justified as strengthening the voluntary sector has subjected this sector to considerable fiscal and emotional strain. In the process, a sharp choice has been posed between two alternative "paradigms" for carrying out this nation's public business. One paradigm, embodied in the enacted and proposed budget changes analyzed here, would significantly reduce the established partnership arrangements between government and nonprofit organizations and seek a sharp separation of the sectors instead. The other paradigm would build on these partnership arrangements and improve them, taking advantage in the process of the complementary advantages of the nonprofit and governmental sectors, the former in the area of service delivery and the latter in the area of funding and democratic priority setting.

How these issues are resolved will go a long way to shaping the character of American society. While there are advantages and disadvantages on both sides, all parties can agree that the issues involved should be scrutinized publicly and analyzed systematically. If this book contributes to such a process, it will have amply served its purpose.

CHAPTER 6

ALTERNATIVES TO THE PRESIDENT'S BUDGET: GRAMM-RUDMAN-HOLLINGS AND SENATE BUDGET RESOLUTION FOR FY 1987

The discussion of federal budget developments of concern to non-profit organizations presented in the previous chapters has focused on the budget changes already enacted in FY 1982-86 and the further changes proposed under the President's new budget for the three years, FY 1987-89. In practice, however, actual federal spending during FY 1987-89 will ultimately be determined not only by what the President proposes or prefers, but by what Congress authorizes and appropriates or by what the automatic provisions of the Gramm-Rudman-Hollings Act specify. Thus, while the President's budget proposal has a central position in the budgetary debate--it represents the most comprehensive, detailed consideration of programs; comes first in the budget season; and goes a long way to structuring subsequent debate--there are other approaches as well to formulating a budget that meets the Gramm-Rudman-Hollings targets.

The purpose of this chapter is to examine the implications for non-profits of the two major alternatives to the President's FY 1987 budget that have surfaced to date--the approach embodied in the automatic provisions of the Gramm-Rudman-Hollings Act and the approach adopted by the Senate in the congressional budget resolution it enacted in May 1986.

Because the level of detail available on these two alternatives is less complete than that available on the president's budget, the analysis here must differ somewhat from that presented in the prior chapters. In particular, instead of program-level detail, data are only available at the level of broad budget "functions." Because of this, it is not possible to spell out the potential direct impacats of the proposed changes on federal support of nonprofits--i.e., the "revenue" analysis. The focus here, therefore, will be on the impacts on overall levels of spending in the fields of interest to nonprofits--i.e., the "demand" analysis. Nevertheless, it is still possible to analyze in broad terms the potential implications for nonprofits of the provisions of the Gramm-Rudman-Hollings Act and those of the Senate budget resolution, and to compare these to the potential implications of the administration's budget proposals.

Gramm-Rudman-Hollings Act

The Balanced Budget and Emergency Deficit Control Act of 1985, the Gramm-Rudman-Hollings Act, set specific deficit targets for each year between FY 1986 and FY 1991 and established an automatic procedure for cutting federal spending to meet these targets in the event that action by the Congress and the president fails to do so. A first set of these automatic cuts went into effect on March 1, 1986, for FY 1986, which was already under way when the act was passed. For the subsequent years, the act established three categories of pograms, as specified in the display below, which provides a general summary of provisions of the Gramm-Rudman-Hollings Act:[1]

---

1. Taken from Congressional Budget Office, The Economic and Budget Outlook: Fiscal Years 1987-1991 (Washington, D.C. Congressional Budget Office, 1986), p. 91.

o <u>Target Deficit Figures</u> (in billions)

FY 1986: $171.9
FY 1987: 144.0
FY 1988: 108.0
FY 1989: 72.0
FY 1990: 36.0
FY 1991: 0.0

o <u>Programs Exempt from Cuts:</u>[2] Total[3] = $592.6 billion

Social Security
Net Interest
Earned Income Tax Credit
Aid to Families with Dependent Chiildren
Child Nutrition
Medicaid
Food Stamps
Supplemental Security Income
Women, Infants, Children Food Supplements
Veterans Compensation and Pensions
State Unemployment Benefits
Offsetting Receipts
Prior Year Outlays and Other

o <u>Programs Partially Exempt from Cuts:</u> Total[3] = $146.5 billion

Civil Service and Military Retirement and Disability
Guaranteed Student Loans
Foster Care and Adoption Assistance
Medicare
Veterans Medical Care
Community Health
Migrant Health
Indian Health

o <u>Programs Subject to Across-the-Board Cuts:</u> Total[3] = $272.2 billion

Defense $171.9
Nondefense[4] 100.3

In the first category are programs like Social Security, Aid to Families with Dependent Children, Medicaid, food stamps, interest on the

---

2. Portions of these programs, such as administrative expenses, may be subject to cuts.

3. FY 1987 outlay estimates used by CBO for making projections on a possible second round (October 1986) of Gramm-Rudman-Hollings cuts. The outlay figures are pre-reduction figures.

4. For a list of selected programs, see table 17.

public debt, and others that are exempt from automatic cuts. In the second category are a set of programs that are not subject to across-the-board cuts, but whose growth can be limited. In the third category are the remaining federal programs, which are subject to across-the-board reductions as needed to meet the target deficit figures. As noted in the display, this third category contains only about one-fourth of all federal spending.

Under the terms of the Gramm-Rudman-Hollings Act, if Congress and the president do not produce a FY 1987 budget by the fall of 1986 that seems likely to produce a federal deficit in the neighborhood of $144 billion, then the Congressional Budget Office and the Office of Management and Budget--at the direction of the comptroller general--must calculate the savings needed out of the third category of programs to achieve the target deficit figure. These required reductions are then split evenly between the defense and nondefense programs included in this third category and across-the-board reductions are applied to both the defense and the nondefense programs.[5]

Because the extent of the Gramm-Rudman-Hollings automatic cuts that will be required for FY 1987 and beyond depends on economic conditions and congressional action that will not be clear until September 1986, it is difficult to predict with precision what the effect of the G-R-H pro-

---

5. Because the defense programs are projected to make up a larger share of the total outlays in this third category of programs in FY 1987, the percentage reductions imposed on each of the defense programs would be lower than that imposed on the nondefense programs. The savings achieved by reductions in the partially exempt programs in the second category lower the amount of across-the-board reductions which are required. For further detail on the Gramm-Rudman-Hollings procedures, see appendix A.

visions will really be. Nevertheless, the Congressional Budget Office (CBO), which advises the Congress on budgeting, has estimated what these automatic cuts might look like given certain economic and budgetary assumptions, and these estimates can be used to gauge the potential impact on nonprofits of the Gramm-Rudman-Hollings provisions, at least for FY 1987.[6]

Table 17 illustrates how these across-the-board Gramm-Rudman-Hollings reductions would affect spending in FY 1987 in a number of programs of particular interest to nonprofits. As this table shows, the Gramm-Rudman-Hollings Act cuts would reduce federal spending by 10 percent or more below FY 1985 levels, even before adjusting for inflation, in such programs as social service block grants, community development block grants, compensatory education, and alcohol, drug abuse, and mental health service grants. With inflation factored in, these cuts are more severe, and when compared to FY 1980 spending levels on these programs, they are even more severe.

To put these potential Gramm-Rudman-Hollings cuts into perspective, however, it is useful to compare them to what is proposed in the president's budget, as is done in table 18. What this table shows is that FY 1987 outlays in the budget functions of greatest interest to nonprofits would be reduced by a smaller amount under Gramm-Rudman-Hollings than under the president's proposals. For the budget function covering education, training, employment, and social service programs,

---

6. Congressional Budget Office, The Economic and Budget Outlook: Fiscal Years 1987-1991 (Washington, D.C.: Congressional Budget Office, 1986), pp. 85-99; and Congressional Budget Office, Reducing the Deficit: Spending and Revenue Options (Washington, D.C.: Congressional Budget Office, 1986), pp. 8-12, 18-20.

Table 17

Estimated Gramm-Rudman-Hollings Cuts for FY 1987
in Selected Federal Programs
(Billions of Dollars unless Otherwise Indicated)

		Percentage Change, Estimated Gramm-Rudman-Hollings FY 1987 Outlays versus:		
Selected Programs	Actual FY 1985 Outlays	FY 1985, Unadjusted for Inflation	FY 1985, After Adjusting for Inflation	FY 1980, After Adjusting for Inflation
Social Service Block Grant	$2,743	-13%	-19%	-38%
Community Services Block Grant	375	-11	-18	-61
Head Start	1,006	-1	-8	-5
Older Workers	320	-4	-11	-9
Community Development Block Grant	3,817	-19	-25	-45
Energy Conservation Grants	464	+1	-6	-11
Chapter 1, Compensatory Education	4,207	-16	-22	-20
Pell Grants and Other Student Aid	4,163	+9	+1	-14
Alcohol, Drug Abuse, Mental Health Services Block Grant	486	-10	-17	-57
Peace Corps	118	-3	-9	-20
National Endowment for the Arts	149	+9	+1	-25

SOURCE: The Urban Institute Nonprofit Sector Project, based on unpublished Office of Management and Budget and Congressional Budget Office documents.

Table 18

Projected Changes in FY 1987 Federal Outlays
in Selected Functions,
Gramm-Rudman-Hollings versus President's FY 1987 Budget versus
Actual FY 1980 Outlays, in Constant FY 1980 Dollars
(Billions of Dollars unless Otherwise Indicated)

Budget Function	Actual FY 1980 Outlays	Projected Change for FY 1987 from FY 1980 Levels		Gramm-Rudman-Hollings Cuts As a Percent of President's Proposed Cuts
		Gramm-Rudman-Hollings	President's Budget	
Education, Training, Employment, and Social Services	$ 31.8	-$10.9	-$12.6	87%
Community and Regional Development	11.3	-6.0	-6.7	90
Health[a]	58.2	+11.5	+8.8	--
Income Assistance	86.5	-0.9	-3.4	26
International Affairs	12.7	-2.7	+0.4	--
Total	$200.5	-$9.0	-$13.5	67%
Total, excluding Medicare, Medicaid	$151.5	-$21.6	-$24.3	89%

SOURCE: Gramm-Rudman estimates based on data in Congressional Budget Office, The Economic and Budget Outlook: Fiscal Years 1987-1991; president's budget projections and actual FY 1980 data from OMB, Budget, FY 1987.

a. Includes Health (function 550) and Medicare (function 570) budget functions, except for Medicare premiums and collections.

for example, federal outlays in FY 1987 would be $10.9 billion below FY 1980 levels under Gramm-Rudman-Hollings compared to $12.6 billion below under the president's proposed budget. In the field of community and regional development, federal outlays would be $6.0 billion below FY 1980 levels under Gramm-Rudman-Hollings compared to $6.7 billion below FY 1980 levels under the administration's proposals. In total, in the five functional areas of interest to nonprofits--excluding Medicare and Medicaid--the Gramm-Rudman-Hollings cuts would be about 89 percent as severe as the reductions proposed in the president's budget.

The central reason Gramm-Rudman-Hollings allows for somewhat more federal spending in these functions than the president's budget is that Gramm-Rudman-Hollings would meet the $144 billion deficit target by making cuts in both defense and nondefense programs, whereas the president's budget proposes to increase defense spending and therefore must impose deeper cuts in the nondefense area, where most of the programs of interest to nonprofits are concentrated. While both approaches would cut programs of interest to nonprofits, therefore, the cuts are somewhat Senate Bud severe under the Gramm-Rudman-Hollings Act approach.

Senate Budget Resolution

In contrast to the Gramm-Rudman-Hollings and administration approaches to reaching the target deficit figure, the Senate adopted a different approach in the budget resolution it enacted on May 2, 1986. Under this resolution, which cleared the Senate by a substantial 70-25 vote margin, the $144 billion deficit target would be reached by freezing most nondefense discretionary spending at FY 1986 levels (that is, permitting no increase for inflation); allowing increased spending for a selected number of "high priority" nondefense programs, such as national science activities, health services for high-risk populations, and certain key educational programs; slowing the growth in defense spending; and increasing the amount of revenues taken in by the federal government.

Table 19 reports the consequences of this strategy for federal spending in a number of budget functions of greatest relevance to non-profit organizations, comparing projected outlays for FY 1987 under both the Senate resolution and the president's budget to what was actually spent in FY 1985. As this table shows, for FY 1987, the Senate budget resolution, like the Gramm-Rudman-Hollings approach, would reduce federal spending less severely than the president's budget. In particular, the Senate's budget resolution would leave the value of federal spending on education, training, employment, and social services only 3 percent lower in FY 1987 than it was in FY 1985, after adjusting for inflation. By contrast, the administration's budget would reduce such spending by 13 percent. Similarly, in the field of community and regional development, the Senate resolution would reduce spending by 13 percent below its FY 1985 level, compared to 22 percent under the President's budget. In fact, in only one of the areas examined here--international affairs--does the Senate budget resolution propose to cut spending more severely than the president's budget, and this is largely because the Senate proposes to spend less than the president for improved security at U.S. embassies, military aid, and foreign broadcast services.

Table 19

Proposed Federal Outlays for FY 1987,
Senate Budget Resolution and President's Budget
Compared to Actual FY 1985 Outlays,
in Constant FY 1985 Dollars
(Billions of Dollars unless Otherwise Indicated)

Function	Actual FY 1985 Outlays	Proposed Changes, FY 1987: Amount: Senate Resolution	Proposed Changes, FY 1987: Amount: President's Budget	Proposed Changes, FY 1987: Percent: Senate Resolution	Proposed Changes, FY 1987: Percent: President's Budget
Education, Training, Employment, and Social Services	$ 29.3	-$0.8	-$3.8	-3%	-13%
Community and Regional Development	7.7	-1.0	-1.7	-13	-22
Health[a]	104.9	-0.4	-4.0	0	-4
Income Assistance	128.2	-15.2	-18.1	-12	-14
International Affairs	16.2	-3.0	+1.1	-19	+ 7
Total	$286.3	-$20.4	-$26.5	-7%	-9%
Total, excluding Medicare, Medicaid	$192.2	-$19.4	-$23.8	-10%	-12%

SOURCE: Senate Budget Committee, "Summary S. Con. Res. 120, Concurrent Resolution on the Budget, FY 1987," Preliminary estimates, May 2, 1986.

a. Includes Health (function 550) and Medicare (function 570), except for Medicare premiums and collections.

While generally resisting presidential proposals for additional cuts in nondefense spending, however, the Senate budget resolution hardly restores federal domestic spending to the levels that existed in FY 1980, prior to the cuts enacted during the first year of the Reagan Administration. This is evident in table 20, which compares projected outlays for FY 1987 under both the Senate budget resolution and the president's budget to what was actually spent in FY 1980, after adjusting for inflation. As this table shows, compared to FY 1980 levels, the Senate resolution endorses only 35 percent of the cuts embodied in the presidet's FY 1987 proposal in the income assistance area, but 93 percent of the cuts proposed in the community and regional development field. Overall, federal spending in FY 1987 in these areas would be cut only 68 percent as much below FY 1980 levels under the Senate budget resolution as under the president's proposals. Excluding Medicare and Medicaid, the cuts embodied in the Senate resoltuion would reduce federal spending by 86 percent as much.

Figure 9 compares what FY 1987 federal spending in selected budget functions would look like in relation to FY 1980 levels under the three versions of the budget being examined here--the president's proposals, the Gramm-Rudman-Hollings provisions, and the budget resolution enacted by the Senate. As this figure shows, under all three versions, defense spending would be much higher in FY 1987 than it was in FY 1980 and spending in fields where nonprofits are active would be much lower. However, the nondefense cuts are less severe under both the Gramm-Rudman-Hollings proposal and the Senate budget resolution than under the president's budget. Of the two alternatives to the president's budget, moreover, the Senate budget resolution extracts somewhat small cuts

Table 20

Projected Changes in FY 1987 Outlays in Selected Functions, Senate Budget Resolution and President's FY 1987 Budget Compared to Actual FY 1980 Outlays, in Constant FY 1980 Dollars (Billions of Dollars unless Otherwise Indicated)

Budget Function	Actual FY 1980 Outlays	Projected Change for FY 1987 from FY 1980 Levels: Senate Budget Resolution	Projected Change for FY 1987 from FY 1980 Levels: President's Budget	Senate Budget Resolution Cuts as a Percent of President's Proposed Cuts for FY 1987
Education, Training, Employment, and Social Services	$ 31.8	-$10.3	-$12.6	82%
Community and Regional Development	11.3	-6.2	-6.7	93
Health[a]	58.2	+11.2	+8.8	--
Income Assistance	86.5	-1.2	-3.4	35
International Affairs	12.7	-2.7	+0.4	--
Total	$200.5	-$ 9.2	-$13.5	68%
Total, excluding Medicare, Medicaid	$151.5	-$21.0	-$24.3	86%

SOURCE: Senate Budget Committee, "Summary, S. Con. Res. 120, Concurrent Resolution on the Budget, FY 1987," preliminary estimates, May 2, 1986; president's budget projections and actual FY 1980 data from OMB, Budget, FY 1987.

a. Includes Health (function 550) and Medicare (function 570) budget functions, except for Medicare premiums and collections.

Figure 9
Proposed Changes in FY 1987 Federal Outlays in Selected Budget Functions Under Three Alternative Budgets*

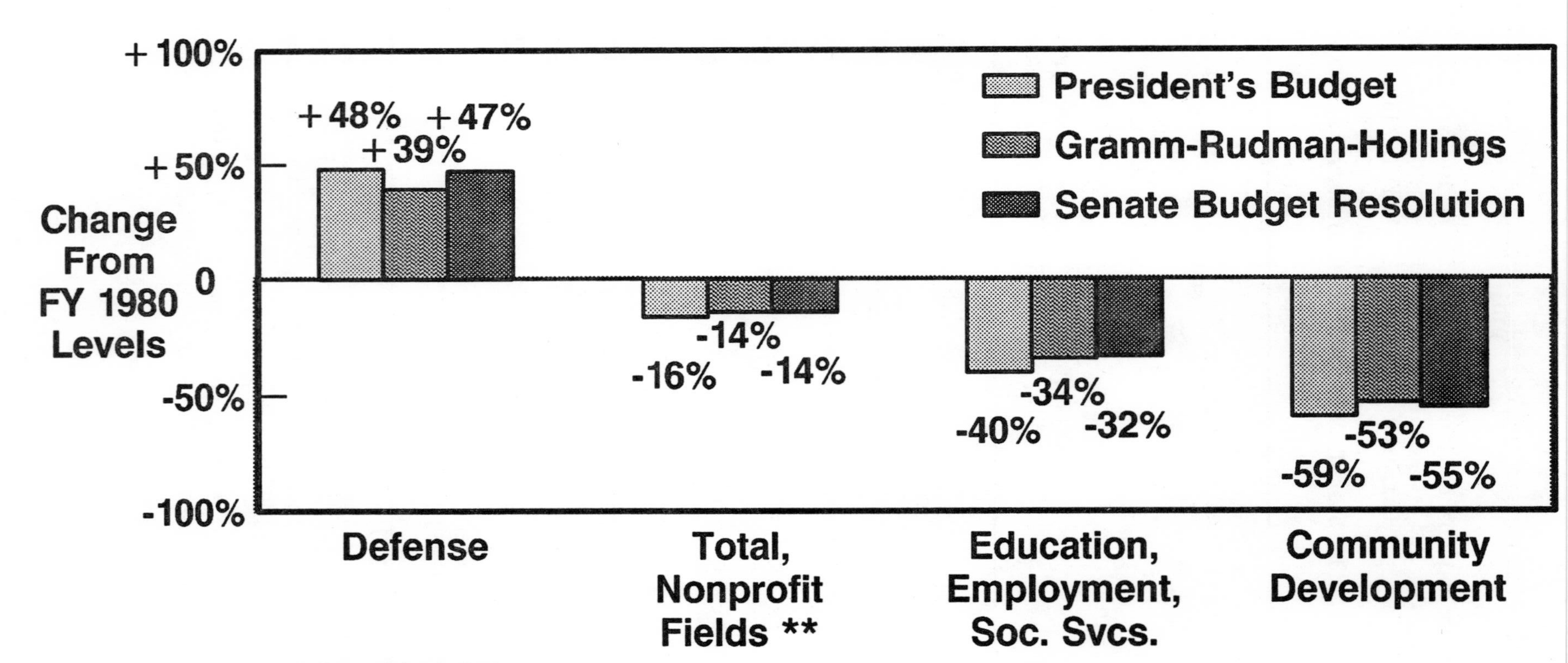

* Adjusted for Inflation

** Excluding Medicare and Medicaid

Source: The Urban Institute Nonprofit Sector Project, Based on OMB and CBO Documents.

out of the important education, employment and training, and social services cluster of programs than does Gramm-Rudman-Hollings; but it cuts slightly more deeply in the community and regional development cluster.

Prospects

Whether actual spending in FY 1987-89 will look more like the president's proposals, the Gramm-Rudman-Hollings projections, or the Senate budget resolution is obviously difficult to say at this point. Because of the requirements of the Gramm-Rudman-Hollings Act, all three approaches are designed to bring the deficit down to $144 billion for FY 1987, and all three involve considerable spending reductions in the programs of interest to nonprofits in order to reach this goal. However, as of this writing, the validity of the Gramm-Rudman-Hollings Act and the strength of the deficit-cutting sentiment which lies behind it are both in question. In the first place, questions about the constitutionality of the Gramm-Rudman-Hollings Act have been raised, with a district court already ruling in February 1986 that the role of the comptroller general in administering the automatic cuts was unconstitutional. Although the Gramm-Rudman-Hollings Act provides for an alternative means of enacting the required cuts legislatively, the Congress and the president may be less willing to follow such a route in the wake of recent, more optimistic deficit projections.

Table 21

Recent Changes in Deficit Estimates
(Billions of Dollars)

Source of Estimate	Deficit Projection FY 1987	FY 1988	FY 1989
Administration's FY 1986 Current Services Estimates	$245.6	$247.8	$232.8
Administration's FY 1987 Current Services Estimates	181.8	150.0	138.9
Deficit Reduction Achieved	$ 63.8	$ 97.8	$ 93.9

SOURCE: Office of Management and Budget, Special Analyses, Budget of the United States Government, Fiscal Year 1986 (Washington, D.C.: Office of Management and Budget, 1985), pp. A-1 to A-44; and OMB, Special Analyses, FY 1987 (Washington, D.C.: OMB, 1986), pp. A-1 to A-44.

These projections show that, in contrast to the increases of the last several years, the deficit is now on a declining path. This is evident in the data recorded in table 21, which compares the deficits projected for FY 1987-89 in the current services estimates the administration made in 1985 with the deficits projected for these same years in the current services estimates it released in February 1986. In its earlier estimates, for example, the administration projected a deficit of $245.6 billion for FY 1987 if no further policy or spending changes were made. In its more recent budget, however, it projects a FY 1987 deficit of only $181.8 billion, declining to $138.9 billion by FY 1989 if no further action is taken.[3] What happened in the year between these

3. Office of Management and Budget, Special Analyses, Budget of the United States Government, Fiscal Year 1986 (Washington, D.C.: Office of Management and Budget, 1985), pp. A-1 to A-44; and OMB, Special

two current services estimates is that actions were taken by the Congress to reduce the deficit--chiefly through reductions in the growth of defense spending, with accompanying reductions in interest charges on the public debt.

Even given this improvement in the underlying deficit picture, further changes are still needed to meet the deficit targets of the Gramm-Rudman-Hollings Act. Thus while the pressures for further deep cuts may lessen somewhat, they are unlikely to disappear. Even if no further cuts are made, moreover, federal spending in the areas of interest to nonprofits and federal support of nonprofits is unlikely to rise back to earlier levels, at least in the foreseeable future. Thus the period of testing for nonprofits, and of challenge for private giving, seems likely to continue.

Appendix A

A GUIDE TO BUDGET CONCEPTS AND PROCEDURES

APPENDIX A

A GUIDE TO BUDGET CONCEPTS AND PROCEDURES

Budget Concepts

Federal budget and spending activities take four quite different forms, reflecting different phases of the spending process. In particular:

- Authorizations: Federal agencies can spend funds only for legally authorized activities. Such authority is what the regular, or "authorizing," committees of Congress provide in passing authorizing legislation. In addition to specifying the uses of public funds, such legislation typically sets upper limits on the amounts that can be devoted to these purposes. Programs can be so authorized for one year (or less) or for multiple years.

- Budget Authority (Appropriations): Although authorizing legislation can set upper bounds on the spending for particular programs, it does not by itself commit actual funds to be used for such purposes, except for one class of programs--the so-called entitlement programs. Entitlement programs are programs like food stamps, Social Security, and veterans assistance, the benefits of which are automatically available to all who meet the eligibility criteria. For these programs, therefore, the amount the government will spend is effectively set by the authorizing committees in the course of defining the eligibility criteria. Entitlement programs account for over 45 percent of total spending.

  For all other programs, the amount available is provided through the "appropriations process," which involves the action of the appropriations committees in Congress and their respective subcommittees. In formal terms, the appropriations process provides agencies with budget authority, to enter into obligations that will lead to the spending of government funds in the same or future years. It represents, in a sense, the checking account balance the program has in the Treasury. Such authority can be provided for a single year or multiple years.

- Obligations: Once programs are authorized and allocated budget authority, agencies may enter into obligations to draw down the budget authority. Obligations are the amounts of orders placed, contracts awarded, services received, and other transactions that require payments, or outlays, in the same or future period.

- Outlays: Neither the granting of budget authority nor the making of obligations by itself involves the actual spending of funds. Rather, a fourth term is used to refer to the actual disbursement of funds: outlays.

  The relationship between budget authority and outlays is one of the trickiest parts of budget making. This relationship differs for different programs depending on the amount of planning involved and the speed with which obligations are made and then translated into actual spending. In some programs, such as the procurement of complex military equipment, obligations are made far in advance of spending, so that actual outlays lag behind obligations and budget authority. Overall, almost 70 percent of budget authority results in outlays in the same year. What this means in practice is that the outlays in any given year may be the result of both budget authority provided in that year and budget authority provided in previous years. Since deficits are measured in terms of actual outlays, this naturally complicates deficit projections as well.

  Under the Reagan budget unveiled in February 1986, a total of $1,102.0 billion of new budget authority was requested for FY 1987. According to administration estimates, this is expected to translate into outlays of $994.0 billion during FY 1987, $253.3 billion of which is to be based on unspent authority from previous years.

In short, authorizations set up programs and may set limits on the amounts of budget authority than can be allocated to them. Budget authority is the amount of money to be spent on a program. Obligations are the amounts of budget authority that have been committed to be spent. Outlays are the monies actually spent.

The Budget Process

The federal budget process now has four major steps: (1) the president's development and submission to Congress of his budget plans, (2) Congress's consideration of the proposals, (3) special deficit reduction activities, and (4) agencies' implementation of the package that is agreed on. The budget process, which last underwent major renovation in 1974, has recently been modified again by the Gramm-Rudman-Hollings Balanced Budget and Emergency Deficit Control Act of 1985. The discussion below incorporates these recent changes. In particular, step three, "deficit reduction," is a product of the Gramm-Rudman-Hollings Act, but the other steps also have been affected by the act.

- Presidential Submissions: At the beginning of every calendar year, the president submits to Congress his proposed budget for the fiscal year beginning the upcoming October 1. The Gramm-Rudman-Hollings Act requires that the president's budget be submitted to Congress on the first Monday after January 3 of each year, although an exception was made for the FY 1987 budget which was allowed to be transmitted in early February.

The president's budget proposal includes detailed projections of budget authority and outlays for the coming and future years, and culminates an executive branch process that begins in the prior spring, some eighteen months before the budget for a particular year is to go into effect. As a consequence of the Gramm-Rudman-Hollings Act, the president's budget must show deficit levels consistent with the target deficit figures set in the Act: $144 billion for FY 1987, $108 billion for FY 1988, $72 billion for FY 1989, $36 billion for FY 1990, and $0 for FY 1991.

In addition to the president's own budget proposals, the president's January submission also contains a current services budget, which indicates the amounts of spending that would be required in the next fiscal year to maintain the same level of government services that is being provided in the current fiscal year, taking into account inflation and other economic and demographic changes.

The current services figures constitute an important element in the formation of a budget, providing a framework against which modifications can be made. They are also a useful tool in appraising a budget: identifying the cuts and additions the proposed budget makes to the current services projections provides a clear indication of where the level of government services can be expected to decrease and increase.

Between January and October, while Congress considers the budget, the president may submit amendments to the original January proposal. When a new president comes in, he typically forwards a set of amendments to Congress. President Reagan did this in February and March 1981. Changes in economic conditions or policy preferences also may lead to amendments.

- Congressional Consideration: Congress receives presidential proposals but can alter them as long as it stays within the deficit targets of Gramm-Rudman-Hollings. Congressional action on the budget takes three different forms: (1) the actions of the authorizing committees in establishing or continuing programs and setting eligibility standards in entitlement programs; (2) the appropriations process, which provides the budget authority agencies need to obligate funds through thirteen separate appropriations bills; and (3) the budget process, which involves a separate set of budget committees that define overall spending targets to which the separate appropriations bills and authorizing legislation must adhere.

By April 15, which is a new, early deadline set by the Gramm-Rudman-Hollings Act, both houses of Congress are supposed to have agreed on a concurrent budget resolution. Presidential approval is not required. The resolution sets targets for outlays and budget authority for the total budget and for the twenty-one functional areas into which federal programs are divided, including national defense; education, training, employment, and social services; and health. The deficit levels in the resolution are supposed to be consistent with the deficit targets indicated in the Gramm-Rudman-Hollings Act. Previously, Congress was also supposed to pass a second binding budget resolution in September of each year but this requirement was rescinded by Gramm-Rudman-Hollings, which instead strengthened the earlier resolution.

Congress considers authorization and appropriations bills in light of the budget resolution, the president's detailed proposals, and the current policy budget, which is the congressional equivalent of the president's current services budget. In addition, the budget resolution may direct Congress to pass reconciliation legislation to bring existing laws in line with the spending levels set in the budget resolution.

The appropriations process is supposed to be completed by October 1, the beginning of the fiscal year. When appropriations bills have not been passed by that date, a continuing resolution must be enacted in order for the government to continue spending money. In no recent year have all appropriations bills been passed on time, so continuing resolutions have been required to continue the funding for at least some agencies.

- Deficit Reduction: As enacted into law in December 1985, the Gramm-Rudman-Hollings Act set up procedures to increase the monitoring of the size of the deficit and to make automatic spending reductions if projected deficits are not sufficiently close--within $10 billion in FY 1987-90--to the deficit targets specified in the act. Among the Gramm-Rudman-Hollings requirements are two discussed above, that the president's budget proposal and the congressional budget resolution contain deficit figures consistent with the Gramm-Rudman-Hollings targets.

  In addition, the Gramm-Rudman-Hollings Act provides that each year on August 15, a month and one-half before the October 1 start of a new fiscal year, the Office of Management and Budget

(OMB) and the Congressional Budget Office (CBO) take a "snapshot" of the projected deficit for the upcoming year.[1]

If the snapshot reveals that in the preceding months Congress and the president have not agreed on actions sufficient to bring the projected deficit down close to the Gramm-Rudman-Hollings target figure, then OMB and CBO transmit to the Comptroller General of the General Accounting Office (GAO) their estimates of the "automatic" cuts required to accomplish the necessary deficit reductions.

The amounts of the automatic cuts are calculated without discretion on the basis of provisions of the Gramm-Rudman-Hollings Act. The act divides federal programs into three categories: those exempt from the cuts; those subject to limited reductions according to "special rules"; and those subject to "across-the-board" reductions. The size of the across-the-board cuts depends on how far the projected deficit is from the target deficit. As provided in the Gramm-Rudman-Hollings Act, defense and non-indexed nondefense programs are required to contribute equal amounts of total outlay savings under the cutting procedures. However, because the amount of defense spending which is eligible for the across-the-board cuts is greater than the amount of nondefense spending which is eligible, the percentage outlay reduction is smaller for defense programs.

Following the August 20 OMB-CBO report to GAO, GAO reviews and revises the report. Several other steps then occur, as indicated in tables A-1 and A-2, culminating in the "sequestration" of funds on October 15 if the projected deficit still remains above the target figures. "Sequestration" involves the permanent cancellation of budget and other spending authority based on a presidential order which must adhere exactly to the GAO-OMB-CBO report.

---

1. A special timetable was used for FY 1986 as indicated in table A-1.

Table A-1

Target Deficits under the
Gramm-Rudman-Hollings Act

Fiscal Year[a]	Maximum Deficit (In billions of dollars)
1986	$171.9
1987	144.0
1988	108.0
1989	72.0
1990	36.0
1991	0.0

SOURCE: U.S. Congressional Budget Office, Reducing the Deficit: Spending and Revenue Options (Washington, D.C.: Congressional Budget Office, 1986), p. 10.

a. Sequestration in 1986 is limited to $11.7 billion. In fiscal years 1987 through 1990, sequestration would be triggered only if the estimated deficit exceeds the maximum by more than $10 billion.

Table A-2

Timetable under The Gramm-Rudman-Hollings Act

Date	Action
	Timetable for Fiscal 1986
January 10	Policy "snapshot" of the deficit for FY 1986 is taken. Laws and regulations as of this date are used for the January 15 report.
January 15	Directors of the Office of Management and Budget (OMB) and the Congressional Budget Office (CBO) report to the comptroller general on the deficit outlook and needed spending cuts.

January 21	Comptroller general issues report to the president, based on the OMB/CBO findings.
February 1	Presidential sequestration order is issued based on the comptroller general's report.
March 1	Sequestration order takes effect.

Timetable for Fiscal 1987 and Thereafter

August 15	Policy "snapshot" of the deficit is taken. Laws and regulations as of this date are used for August 20 report.
August 20	Directors of OMB and CBO report to the comptroller general on deficit outlook and needed spending cuts.
August 25	Comptroller general issues report to the president.
September 1	If a sequestration is called for, the initial presidential order is issued based on the comptroller general's report.
October 1	Initial order takes effect; sequestered funds are withheld from obligation.
October 5	Directors of OMB and CBO issue revised report to reflect final congressional action on efforts to reduce the deficit.
October 10	Comptroller general issues revised report to the president.
October 15	If sequestration is still necessary, the final presidential order, based on the revised report, is effective; sequestered funds are permanently canceled.

SOURCE: U.S. Congressional Budget Office, Reducing the Deficit: Spending and Revenue Options (Washington, D.C.: Congressional Budget Office, 1986), p. 10.

Although the constitutionality of the automatic Gramm-Rudman-Hollings spending cut procedures is now under Supreme Court review, the act provides alternative fallback procedures for accomplishing the necessary cuts by a more normal legislative route, in which the Congress would pass and the president would sign a bill incorporating the cuts.

o Implementation and Modifications: Budget authority provided to programs in the appropriations process is obligated by agencies during the fiscal year according to an apportionment schedule set by the director of the Office of Management and Budget.

Occasionally supplemental appropriations may be desired or required, especially for entitlement programs.

When the president wants to cut money being spent in the current fiscal year, he may seek to defer spending. Under the Congressional Budget Act of 1974, presidential deferrals could be overruled by either house of Congress. However, since the one-house legislative veto has been invalidated by the Supreme Court, there is now some question about the status of the deferral procedure.

Budget authority can be canceled by the passage of a rescission bill. Unless Congress approves a rescission bill within forty-five days after it has been proposed by the president, the budget authority in question must be made available for obligation.

REFERENCES: U.S. General Accounting Office, A Glossary of Terms Used in the Federal Budget Process, 3d ed. (Washington, D.C.: U.S. General Accounting Office, 1981); and U.S. Office of Management and Budget, Budget of the United States Government, Fiscal Year 1987 (Washington, D.C.: Office of Management and Budget, 1986) pp. 6b-1 to 6b-6.

APPENDIX B

OUTLAYS BY PROGRAM IN FY 1980 DOLLARS

This appendix records past outlays and those proposed for FY 1987-89 for programs of interest to nonprofits after adjusting for inflation using the CPI-medical deflator for health finance programs and the GNP-implicit price deflator for all other programs. Actual deflators are used for FY 1980-85 and Office of Management and Budget projections for the deflators are used for FY 1986-89.

APPENDIX B

INFLATION-ADJUSTED

FEDERAL OUTLAYS FOR PROGRAMS OF INTEREST TO NONPROFITS,
UNDER THE FEBRUARY 1986 VERSION OF PRESIDENT REAGAN'S FY 1987 BUDGET,
ENACTED FY 1980-85 OUTLAYS, ESTIMATES FOR FY 1986, AND PROPOSALS FOR FY 1987-89,
IN MILLIONS OF CONSTANT FY 1980 DOLLARS[a]

	ENACTED						EST.	PROPOSED		
SOCIAL WELFARE PROGRAMS	FY 1980	FY 1981	FY 1982	FY 1983	FY 1984	FY 1985	FY 1986	FY 1987	FY 1988	FY 1989
SOCIAL SERVICES SUBAREA										
SOCIAL SERVICES BLOCK GRANT[b]	2706	2557	2149	2023	2181	2071	1903	1890	1825	1765
CHILD WELFARE SERVICES	64	164	137	130	135	145	148	143	138	133
FOSTER CARE	263	298	219	288	376	411	449	429	425	437
COMMUNITY SERVICES BLOCK GRANT[b]	592	563	328	271	271	283	170	44	0	0
REHABILITATION SERVICES	956	907	661	771	1106	602	1046	841	829	796
SOCIAL SERVICES OTHER GROUPS	101	89	77	71	70	75	75	70	68	65
HEAD START	737	696	706	717	717	759	758	741	724	703
SOCIAL SERVICES FOR ELDERLY	679	660	530	512	549	528	492	479	465	450
DOMESTIC VOLUNTEERS	133	136	115	102	104	97	117	105	102	101
HOUSING COUNSELING ASSISTANCE	8	5	3	2	2	2	3	0	0	0
OTHER SOCIAL SERVICES	8	6	22	12	16	16	18	14	14	13
CRIMINAL JUSTICE ASSISTANCE	650	430	249	136	106	113	156	148	88	80
LEGAL SERVICES	320	295	219	190	212	226	220	27	0	0
OTHER HUMAN DEVPT, FAMILY SERVICES	128	112	73	85	91	88	89	85	84	80
TOTAL--SOCIAL SERVICES	7345	6917	5489	5311	5935	5419	5641	5016	4760	4624
EMPLOYMENT, TRAINING SUBAREA										
TRAINING PROGRAMS[c]	2835	2665	2225	2069	1507	1545	1668	1557	1452	1392
YOUTH TRAINING PROGRAMS	2330	2153	1058	1067	992	1033	1015	628	578	513
PUBLIC SERVICE EMPLOYMENT	3697	2181	232	37	-12	-14	0	0	0	0
OLDER WORKERS	235	239	228	223	251	242	236	221	220	213
WORK INCENTIVE PROGRAM	395	346	199	235	207	211	132	18	5	0
FED-STATE EMPLOYMENT SERVICE	756	731	619	602	625	693	719	667	647	641
TRAINING PROGRAM ADMIN	97	85	68	72	61	43	45	46	43	42
VA VETERANS JOB TRAINING	0	0	0	0	13	52	36	4	0	0
TOTAL--EMPLOYMENT, TRAINING	10345	8400	4630	4304	3644	3805	3851	3139	2946	2800

APPENDIX B (cont.)

INFLATION-ADJUSTED

COMMUNITY DEVELOPMENT SUBAREA	ENACTED						EST.	PROPOSED		
	FY 1980	FY 1981	FY 1982	FY 1983	FY 1984	FY 1985	FY 1986	FY 1987	FY 1988	FY 1989
COMMUNITY ECONOMIC DEVELOPMENT	50	0	0	0	0	0	0	0	0	0
COMMUNITY DEVELOPMENT BLOCK GRANT	3902	3674	3213	2889	2986	2881	2612	2175	1777	1741
URBAN DEVELOPMENT ACTION GRANT	225	337	329	367	355	375	357	290	224	140
SEC 312 REHABILITATION LOANS	165	55	-19	-27	-16	-7	-2	-46	-51	-49
NEIGHBORHOOD REINVESTMENT CORPORATION	12	11	12	13	13	12	13	11	11	10
PENNSYLVANIA AVENUE DEVELOPMENT CORPORATION	24	32	22	12	11	8	9	10	5	3
URBAN PLANNING ASSISTANCE	40	35	17	2	0	0	1	0	0	0
OTHER COMMUNITY DEVELOPMENT	511	454	286	215	141	117	151	131	103	97
FMHA RURAL DEVELOPMENT[d]	1791	1694	1675	1255	1206	1258	1188	1125	1096	891
ECONOMIC DEVELOPMENT ASSISTANCE	629	487	349	246	162	265	164	122	81	41
INDIAN COMMUNITY DEVELOPMENT	991	894	913	906	866	796	785	807	780	759
REGIONAL COMMISSIONS	458	386	289	227	173	165	118	90	59	33
OTHER REGIONAL DEVELOPMENT	164	185	164	128	135	106	102	76	71	42
HOUSING FOR ELDERLY OR HANDICAPPED	753	743	629	650	517	378	358	270	176	116
RURAL HOUSING[d]	3625	3560	3429	2914	2682	2998	2424	1186	1005	717
NEIGHBORHOOD SELF-HELP DEVELOPMENT	15	8	3	0	0	0	0	0	0	0
ENERGY CONSERVATION GRANTS	372	436	439	387	406	350	317	180	145	85
SOLAR ENERGY AND ENERGY CONSERVATION BANK	0	0	0	0	6	20	26	6	0	0
RENTAL REHABILITATION GRANTS	0	0	0	0	0	11	102	95	7	0
EMERGENCY FOOD AND SHELTER	0	0	0	64	45	52	66	0	0	0
RENTAL DEVELOPMENT GRANTS	0	0	0	0	0	1	75	74	70	0
TOTAL--COMMUNITY DEVELOPMENT	13727	12991	11751	10249	9688	9785	8866	6602	5558	4627
TOTAL--SOCIAL WELFARE	31417	28309	21871	19865	19268	19008	18358	14757	13265	12052

APPENDIX B (cont.)

INFLATION-ADJUSTED

EDUCATION, RESEARCH AND DEVELOPMENT PROGRAMS	ENACTED						EST.	PROPOSED		
	FY 1980	FY 1981	FY 1982	FY 1983	FY 1984	FY 1985	FY 1986	FY 1987	FY 1988	FY 1989
ELEMENTARY, SECONDARY EDUCATION SUBAREA										
INDIAN EDUCATION	395	287	287	273	258	286	262	222	220	212
IMPACT AID	690	634	463	445	452	488	519	429	383	361
EDUCATION FOR HANDICAPPED	822	941	967	1049	745	768	1103	885	905	845
VOCATIONAL AND ADULT EDUCATION	863	662	693	584	581	497	722	576	408	342
OTHER ELEMENTARY AND SECONDARY EDUCATION	30	4	15	20	17	16	23	17	16	16
COMPENSATORY EDUCATION BLOCK GRANT[b]	3095	3049	2503	2151	2406	3176	2156	2482	2509	2410
STATE EDUCATION BLOCK GRANT[b]	913	669	636	450	494	397	482	435	448	443
BILINGUAL EDUCATION	159	157	142	133	131	119	93	109	97	94
TOTAL--ELEMENTARY, SECONDARY EDUCATION	6967	6402	5706	5103	5084	5747	5359	5155	4986	4723
HIGHER EDUCATION SUBAREA										
STUDENT FINANCIAL ASSISTANCE	3683	3551	2315	3288	2927	3143	3646	2993	2384	2304
STUDENT LOAN GUARANTEES	1408	2053	2562	2078	2537	2669	2361	1787	1416	1369
HIGHER AND CONTINUING EDUCATION[d]	410	380	373	299	140	186	331	201	46	82
SPECIAL INSTITUTIONS	193	187	176	183	120	181	197	160	156	148
VETERANS EDUCATIONAL BENEFITS	2342	2049	1650	1321	1049	793	427	385	378	350
SOCIAL SECURITY STUDENT BENEFITS	1559	1819	1251	593	172	26	0	0	0	0
NIH HEALTH TRAINING	193	191	165	158	152	176	204	189	174	168
OTHER HEALTH TRAINING	526	517	403	312	152	177	129	63	20	20
SEA GRANTS	36	37	31	27	27	29	6	0	0	0
TOTAL--HIGHER EDUCATION	10350	10784	8926	8259	7277	7381	7300	5779	4574	4441
RESEARCH AND DEVELOPMENT SUBAREA[e]										
DEPT OF DEFENSE R & D	578	611	661	735	795	901	923	976	1090	1106
DEPT OF HEALTH AND HUMAN SERVICES R & D	2423	2510	2385	2283	2417	2608	2823	2686	2622	2466
DEPT OF AGRICULTURE R & D	160	171	199	196	196	193	196	193	189	174
NATIONAL SCIENCE FOUNDATION R & D	687	668	698	658	736	769	836	878	878	879
DEPT OF ENERGY R & D	340	347	333	298	299	300	282	270	278	282
NASA R & D	209	212	129	98	108	112	117	118	114	116
EPA R & D	61	49	36	28	28	26	31	32	28	29
DEPT OF INTERIOR R & D	55	55	49	40	38	39	36	32	31	30
VETERANS ADMINISTRATION R & D	3	3	3	3	4	4	4	4	3	3
DEPT OF EDUCATION R & D	59	42	53	37	95	17	37	34	36	35
NUCLEAR REGULATORY COMMISSION R & D	25	25	25	28	23	23	20	19	18	18
DEPT OF TRANSPORTATION R & D	27	26	19	15	20	29	27	20	16	14
DEPT OF COMMERCE R & D	54	43	36	41	44	48	47	37	37	34
DEPT OF HOUSING AND URBAN DEVELOPMENT R & D	15	11	7	5	5	4	4	4	3	3
TOTAL--RESEARCH AND DEVELOPMENT	4696	4772	4633	4467	4809	5074	5382	5302	5344	5189
TOTAL--EDUCATION, RESEARCH AND DEVELOPMENT	22013	21959	19265	17829	17170	18201	18041	16235	14904	14353

APPENDIX B (cont.)

INFLATION-ADJUSTED

	ENACTED						EST.	PROPOSED		
HEALTH PROGRAMS	FY 1980	FY 1981	FY 1982	FY 1983	FY 1984	FY 1985	FY 1986	FY 1987	FY 1988	FY 1989
HEALTH FINANCE SUBAREA										
MEDICARE[f]	35034	38508	40838	41932	43338	46664	45879	45269	46908	49168
MEDICAID	14028	15360	14130	14058	13988	14839	15263	14472	14295	14285
FEDERAL EMPLOYEE HEALTH BENEFITS	608	731	753	752	931	798	420	399	642	648
TOTAL--HEALTH FINANCE	49670	54599	55720	56742	58256	62301	61563	60139	61845	64100
HEALTH SERVICES SUBAREA										
HEALTH RESOURCES AND SVCS ADMIN HEALTH SERVICES	310	278	366	249	173	184	160	34	90	82
INDIAN HEALTH SERVICES	549	536	499	509	563	620	543	510	490	474
INDIAN HEALTH FACILITIES	87	81	55	54	54	38	48	26	9	2
PREVENTIVE HEALTH SERVICES	160	150	143	163	167	159	202	195	187	181
ALCOHOL, DRUG ABUSE, MENTAL HEALTH SERVICES	128	156	58	73	84	53	16	30	23	18
OTHER HEALTH SERVICES	369	375	209	161	112	109	122	114	109	110
PREVENTIVE HEALTH SERVICES BLOCK GRANT[b]	194	107	107	87	70	72	62	62	60	58
ALCOHOL, DRUG ABUSE, MENTAL HEALTH BLOCK GRANT[b]	708	604	556	411	392	367	344	340	331	320
PRIMARY CARE BLOCK GRANT[b]	484	484	457	352	450	435	438	397	382	369
MATERNAL AND CHILD HEALTH BLOCK GRANT[b]	361	362	437	347	318	305	358	332	323	312
TOTAL--HEALTH SERVICES	3350	3132	2888	2406	2382	2342	2294	2041	2004	1927
TOTAL--HEALTH	53020	57732	58608	59148	60638	64643	63857	62180	63849	66027

APPENDIX B (cont.)

INFLATION-ADJUSTED

INCOME ASSISTANCE PROGRAMS	ENACTED						EST.	PROPOSED		
	FY 1980	FY 1981	FY 1982	FY 1983	FY 1984	FY 1985	FY 1986	FY 1987	FY 1988	FY 1989
HOUSING ASSISTANCE SUBAREA										
FARM LABOR HOUSING	13	15	17	13	9	2	7	8	7	5
MUTUAL AND SELF-HELP HOUSING	6	6	7	6	6	6	5	6	3	2
NONPROFIT SPONSOR HOUSING ASSISTANCE	0	0	0	0	0	0	0	0	-1	0
SUBSIDIZED HOUSING[g]	4529	5224	5830	6329	6860	7544	7776	7427	7438	7517
OTHER HOUSING[g]	932	994	980	1330	981	996	1122	1016	968	968
TOTAL--HOUSING ASSISTANCE	5480	6240	6833	7678	7857	8549	8910	8458	8416	8492
CASH ASSISTANCE SUBAREA										
SUPPLEMENTAL SECURITY INCOME	6411	6538	6505	7092	6645	7252	7425	7396	7935	7402
AID TO FAMILIES WITH DEPENDENT CHILDREN	7045	7432	6771	6822	6924	6963	7116	6271	6616	6566
EARNED INCOME TAX CREDIT	1275	1198	1018	986	933	830	937	862	751	703
TOTAL--CASH ASSISTANCE	14731	15168	14294	14900	14501	15045	15478	14529	15303	14671
FOOD ASSISTANCE SUBAREA										
FOOD STAMPS	9117	10229	9333	10286	9676	9456	9125	8655	8578	8460
WOMEN, INFANTS, CHILDREN FOOD SUPPLEMENTS	717	845	788	935	1093	1161	1182	1160	1128	1132
CHILD AND OTHER NUTRITION	4181	3653	3082	3308	3302	3327	3314	2887	2932	3012
TOTAL--FOOD ASSISTANCE	14015	14728	13203	14528	14071	13944	13622	12702	12637	12603
OTHER INCOME ASSISTANCE SUBAREA										
REFUGEE ASSISTANCE	368	660	857	426	471	334	287	241	249	226
LOW INCOME ENERGY ASSISTANCE	1577	1618	1430	1620	1584	1616	1475	1468	1419	1373
OTHER INCOME ASSISTANCE	223	184	158	190	190	146	119	101	94	92
TOTAL--OTHER INCOME ASSISTANCE	2168	2462	2445	2236	2245	2096	1882	1810	1762	1690
TOTAL--INCOME ASSISTANCE	36394	38597	36775	39342	38674	39634	39892	37498	38118	37456

APPENDIX B (cont.)

INFLATION-ADJUSTED

	ENACTED						EST.	PROPOSED		
FOREIGN AID PROGRAMS	FY 1980	FY 1981	FY 1982	FY 1983	FY 1984	FY 1985	FY 1986	FY 1987	FY 1988	FY 1989
AGENCY FOR INTERNATIONAL DEVELOPMENT	1428	1403	1277	1347	1391	1456	1529	1463	1406	1356
MULTILATERAL DEVELOPMENT BANKS	784	868	901	1010	1088	1077	869	1105	1058	884
PUBLIC LAW 480 FOOD ASSISTANCE	1073	1140	787	806	848	1295	1003	813	794	779
PEACE CORPS	101	90	87	89	87	89	90	88	85	84
ECONOMIC SUPPORT AND PEACEKEEPING	1904	1893	2069	2212	2278	3719	3545	2875	2926	2790
REFUGEE ASSISTANCE	446	349	324	259	263	291	251	239	233	218
INTERNATIONAL ORGANIZATIONS AND CONFERENCES	492	401	461	392	454	408	376	342	318	315
FOREIGN INFORMATION AND EXCHANGE	534	477	484	489	533	599	680	732	757	798
OTHER INTERNATIONAL DEVELOPMENT ASSISTANCE	182	240	148	99	171	196	186	131	108	103
TOTAL--FOREIGN AID	6944	6861	6538	6704	7112	9128	8529	7788	7686	7329
ARTS AND CULTURE PROGRAMS										
CORPORATION FOR PUBLIC BROADCASTING	152	147	146	111	108	113	117	140	115	85
NATIONAL ENDOWMENT FOR THE ARTS	152	135	114	102	113	112	126	114	100	95
NATIONAL ENDOWMENT FOR THE HUMANITIES	168	151	116	109	109	113	108	91	86	83
SMITHSONIAN AND OTHER INSTITUTIONS	160	169	164	176	165	171	175	181	178	171
INSTITUTE OF MUSEUM SERVICES	13	0	24	7	13	14	19	11	0	0
TOTAL--ARTS AND CULTURE	645	603	563	506	509	525	545	538	479	434
ENVIRONMENT AND CONSERVATION PROGRAMS										
URBAN PARK AND RECREATION GRANTS	4	16	27	23	30	33	10	3	1	0
YOUTH CONSERVATION CORPS	60	25	5	0	0	0	0	0	0	0
FEDERAL LAND ACQUISITION	595	450	296	268	246	265	191	138	49	41
HISTORIC PRESERVATION FUND	49	48	31	25	40	22	13	2	1	0
TOTAL--ENVIRONMENT	708	539	359	316	316	320	215	143	51	41
OTHER PROGRAMS										
NONPROFIT MAIL SUBSIDY[h]	276	271	229	223	232	261	216	0	0	0
OTHER MAIL SUBSIDY[i]	477	493	390	376	375	432	331	0	0	0
TOTAL--OTHER	753	764	619	599	607	693	547	0	0	0
GRAND TOTAL--ALL PROGRAMS	151894	155363	144597	144309	144293	152152	149985	139139	138352	137692

APPENDIX B (cont.)

Source: U.S. Office of Management and Budget, Budget of the United States Government, FY 1987 and preceding years, unpublished backup material; and other unpublished executive branch agency and Congressional budget material.

a. Health finance program outlays have been deflated by the CPI-medical care deflator. All other program outlays have been deflated by the GNP-implicit price deflator. Actual fiscal year deflators were used for FY 1980-85, and Office of Management and Budget fiscal year projections were used for FY 1986-89. Both actual and projected deflators were obtained from unpublished Office of Management and Budget material.

b. The current program was created by the Omnibus Budget Reconciliation Act of 1981. Outlay figures include spending for preexisting programs which covered the same activities.

c. The Job Training Partnership Act (JTPA) replaced the Comprehensive Employment and Training Act (CETA) in 1982.

d. Outlay figures do not include the effects of the enacted or proposed sale of loan assets.

e. Included in research and development outlays is the federal spending on research and development which goes outside the government to public and private, nonprofit colleges and universities and nonprofit research institutes. Intramural government spending and support going to for-profit businesses are not included.

f. Excludes revenues from Medicare premiums and collections.

g. Outlay figures exclude outlays in the public housing loan account and related proposed outlays in the subsidized housing account.

h. Outlay figures include the estimated Treasury subsidy for reduced mail rates for private, nonprofit organizations. The President's FY 1987 budget proposes to end the Treasury reimbursement to the Postal Service for subsidized mail rates, although the budget indicates that legislation will be proposed to allow the Postal Service to continue the subsidy on its own.

i. Outlay figures include the estimated Treasury subsidy for reduced mail rates for public, for-profit, and religious organizations. Also see note h.

APPENDIX C

OUTLAYS BY PROGRAM IN CURRENT DOLLARS

This appendix records past outlays and those proposed for FY 1987-89 for programs of interest to nonprofits without any adjustment for inflation.

APPENDIX C

CURRENT DOLLARS

FEDERAL OUTLAYS FOR PROGRAMS OF INTEREST TO NONPROFITS,
UNDER THE FEBRUARY 1986 VERSION OF PRESIDENT REAGAN'S FY 1987 BUDGET,
ENACTED FY 1980-85 OUTLAYS, ESTIMATES FOR FY 1986, AND PROPOSALS FOR FY 1987-89,
IN MILLIONS OF CURRENT DOLLARS

	ENACTED						EST.	PROPOSED		
SOCIAL WELFARE PROGRAMS	FY 1980	FY 1981	FY 1982	FY 1983	FY 1984	FY 1985	FY 1986	FY 1987	FY 1988	FY 1989
SOCIAL SERVICES SUBAREA										
SOCIAL SERVICES BLOCK GRANT[a]	2706	2813	2536	2489	2789	2743	2604	2693	2700	2700
CHILD WELFARE SERVICES	64	180	162	160	173	192	202	203	204	204
FOSTER CARE	263	328	259	354	481	545	614	611	629	669
COMMUNITY SERVICES BLOCK GRANT[a]	592	619	387	333	346	375	232	62	0	0
REHABILITATION SERVICES	956	998	780	949	1414	798	1432	1198	1226	1218
SOCIAL SERVICES OTHER GROUPS	101	98	91	87	89	99	102	100	100	100
HEAD START	737	766	833	882	917	1006	1037	1056	1072	1075
SOCIAL SERVICES FOR ELDERLY	679	726	626	630	702	700	673	683	688	689
DOMESTIC VOLUNTEERS	133	150	136	126	133	129	160	149	151	154
HOUSING COUNSELING ASSISTANCE	8	5	3	3	3	3	4	0	0	0
OTHER SOCIAL SERVICES	8	7	26	15	21	21	24	20	20	20
CRIMINAL JUSTICE ASSISTANCE	650	473	294	167	136	150	213	211	130	122
LEGAL SERVICES	320	324	259	234	271	300	301	38	0	0
OTHER HUMAN DEVPT, FAMILY SERVICES	128	123	86	105	116	117	122	121	124	123
TOTAL--SOCIAL SERVICES	7345	7610	6478	6534	7591	7178	7720	7145	7044	7074
EMPLOYMENT, TRAINING SUBAREA										
TRAINING PROGRAMS[b]	2835	2932	2626	2545	1927	2046	2283	2218	2149	2129
YOUTH TRAINING PROGRAMS	2330	2369	1249	1313	1269	1369	1389	894	856	785
PUBLIC SERVICE EMPLOYMENT	3697	2399	274	45	-15	-18	0	0	0	0
OLDER WORKERS	235	263	269	274	321	320	323	315	326	326
WORK INCENTIVE PROGRAM	395	381	235	289	265	279	180	25	8	0
FEDERAL-STATE EMPLOYMENT SERVICE	756	804	731	741	799	918	984	950	958	980
TRAINING PROGRAM ADMINISTRATION	97	93	80	88	78	57	62	65	63	64
VA VETERANS JOB TRAINING	0	0	0	0	17	69	49	5	0	0
TOTAL--EMPLOYMENT, TRAINING	10345	9241	5464	5295	4661	5040	5270	4472	4360	4284

APPENDIX C (cont.)

CURRENT DOLLARS

COMMUNITY DEVELOPMENT SUBAREA	ENACTED						EST.	PROPOSED		
	FY 1980	FY 1981	FY 1982	FY 1983	FY 1984	FY 1985	FY 1986	FY 1987	FY 1988	FY 1989
COMMUNITY ECONOMIC DEVELOPMENT	50	0	0	0	0	0	0	0	0	0
COMMUNITY DEVELOPMENT BLOCK GRANT	3902	4042	3792	3554	3819	3817	3575	3099	2629	2664
URBAN DEVELOPMENT ACTION GRANT	225	371	388	451	454	497	488	413	331	214
SEC 312 REHABILITATION LOANS	165	60	-23	-33	-21	-9	-3	-65	-75	-75
NEIGHBORHOOD REINVESTMENT CORPORATION	12	12	14	16	16	16	18	15	16	16
PENNSYLVANIA AVENUE DEVELOPMENT CORPORATION	24	35	26	15	14	10	13	14	7	4
URBAN PLANNING ASSISTANCE	40	39	20	3	0	0	1	0	0	0
OTHER COMMUNITY DEVELOPMENT	511	499	338	264	180	155	206	186	152	148
FMHA RURAL DEVELOPMENT[c]	1791	1864	1977	1544	1543	1666	1626	1603	1622	1363
ECONOMIC DEVELOPMENT ASSISTANCE	629	536	412	303	207	351	225	174	120	63
INDIAN COMMUNITY DEVELOPMENT	991	984	1078	1114	1108	1054	1074	1149	1154	1161
REGIONAL COMMISSIONS	458	425	341	279	221	218	161	128	88	51
OTHER REGIONAL DEVELOPMENT	164	203	193	158	173	140	139	108	105	64
HOUSING FOR ELDERLY OR HANDICAPPED	753	817	742	800	661	501	490	385	260	178
RURAL HOUSING[c]	3625	3916	4047	3585	3430	3971	3318	1690	1487	1097
NEIGHBORHOOD SELF-HELP DEVELOPMENT	15	9	4	0	0	0	0	0	0	0
ENERGY CONSERVATION GRANTS	372	480	518	476	519	464	434	256	215	130
SOLAR ENERGY AND ENERGY CONSERVATION BANK	0	0	0	0	8	27	36	9	0	0
RENTAL REHABILITATION GRANTS	0	0	0	0	0	14	140	136	10	0
EMERGENCY FOOD AND SHELTER	0	0	0	79	58	69	90	0	0	0
RENTAL DEVELOPMENT GRANTS	0	0	0	0	0	1	103	105	104	0
TOTAL--COMMUNITY DEVELOPMENT	13727	14292	13867	12608	12390	12962	12134	9405	8225	7078
TOTAL--SOCIAL WELFARE	31417	31143	25809	24437	24642	25180	25124	21022	19629	18436

APPENDIX C (cont.)

CURRENT DOLLARS

EDUCATION, RESEARCH AND DEVELOPMENT PROGRAMS	ENACTED FY 1980	FY 1981	FY 1982	FY 1983	FY 1984	FY 1985	EST. FY 1986	PROPOSED FY 1987	FY 1988	FY 1989
ELEMENTARY, SECONDARY EDUCATION SUBAREA										
INDIAN EDUCATION	395	316	339	336	330	379	358	316	325	325
IMPACT AID	690	697	546	548	578	647	710	611	566	552
EDUCATION FOR HANDICAPPED	822	1035	1141	1290	953	1018	1509	1261	1339	1292
VOCATIONAL AND ADULT EDUCATION	863	728	818	718	743	658	988	820	604	523
OTHER ELEMENTARY AND SECONDARY EDUCATION	30	4	18	24	22	21	31	24	24	24
COMPENSATORY EDUCATION BLOCK GRANT[a]	3095	3354	2954	2646	3077	4207	2951	3536	3713	3687
STATE EDUCATION BLOCK GRANT[a]	913	736	751	553	632	526	660	620	663	678
BILINGUAL EDUCATION	159	173	167	163	167	157	127	155	144	144
TOTAL--ELEMENTARY, SECONDARY EDUCATION	6967	7043	6734	6278	6502	7613	7334	7343	7378	7225
HIGHER EDUCATION SUBAREA										
STUDENT FINANCIAL ASSISTANCE	3683	3906	2732	4045	3743	4163	4990	4264	3528	3524
STUDENT LOAN GUARANTEES	1408	2259	3023	2556	3245	3535	3231	2546	2095	2094
HIGHER AND CONTINUING EDUCATION[c]	410	418	440	368	179	246	453	287	68	125
SPECIAL INSTITUTIONS	193	206	208	225	154	240	269	228	231	227
VETERANS EDUCATIONAL BENEFITS	2342	2254	1947	1625	1342	1051	584	548	559	536
SOCIAL SECURITY STUDENT BENEFITS	1559	2001	1476	730	220	35	0	0	0	0
NIH HEALTH TRAINING	193	210	195	194	195	233	279	269	257	257
OTHER HEALTH TRAINING	526	569	475	384	194	235	176	90	30	31
SEA GRANTS	36	41	37	33	35	39	8	0	0	0
TOTAL--HIGHER EDUCATION	10350	11864	10533	10160	9307	9777	9990	8232	6768	6794
RESEARCH AND DEVELOPMENT SUBAREA[d]										
DEPT OF DEFENSE R & D	578	672	780	904	1017	1193	1263	1391	1613	1692
DEPT OF HEALTH AND HUMAN SERVICES R & D	2423	2761	2815	2808	3091	3455	3863	3826	3880	3773
DEPT OF AGRICULTURE R & D	160	188	235	241	251	256	268	275	279	266
NATIONAL SCIENCE FOUNDATION R & D	687	735	824	810	941	1019	1144	1250	1299	1344
DEPT OF ENERGY R & D	340	382	393	367	382	398	386	384	411	431
NASA R & D	209	233	152	121	138	149	160	168	169	178
EPA R & D	61	54	43	35	36	35	43	45	42	44
DEPT OF INTERIOR R & D	55	60	58	49	48	52	49	46	46	46
VETERANS ADMINISTRATION R & D	3	3	3	4	5	5	5	5	5	5
DEPT OF EDUCATION R & D	59	46	62	46	122	22	50	49	53	53
NUCLEAR REGULATORY COMMISSION R & D	25	28	29	34	30	31	28	27	27	27
DEPT OF TRANSPORTATION R & D	27	29	22	19	26	38	37	28	24	22
DEPT OF COMMERCE R & D	54	47	43	51	56	63	65	53	55	52
DEPT OF HOUSING AND URBAN DEVELOPMENT R & D	15	12	8	6	7	5	5	5	5	5
TOTAL--RESEARCH AND DEVELOPMENT	4696	5250	5467	5495	6150	6721	7366	7552	7908	7938
TOTAL--EDUCATION, RESEARCH AND DEVELOPMENT	22013	24157	22734	21933	21959	24111	24690	23127	22054	21957

APPENDIX C (cont.)

CURRENT DOLLARS

HEALTH PROGRAMS	ENACTED						EST.	PROPOSED		
	FY 1980	FY 1981	FY 1982	FY 1983	FY 1984	FY 1985	FY 1986	FY 1987	FY 1988	FY 1989
HEALTH FINANCE SUBAREA										
MEDICARE[e]	35034	42489	50423	56841	62482	71384	74431	77528	84963	93850
MEDICAID	14028	16948	17446	19057	20167	22700	24762	24785	25892	27266
FEDERAL EMPLOYEE HEALTH BENEFITS	608	807	930	1019	1342	1221	682	683	1162	1236
TOTAL--HEALTH FINANCE	49670	60244	68799	76917	83991	95305	99875	102996	112017	122352
HEALTH SERVICES SUBAREA										
HEALTH RESOURCES AND SVCS ADMIN HEALTH SERVICES	310	306	432	306	221	244	219	49	133	125
INDIAN HEALTH SERVICES	549	590	589	626	720	821	743	726	725	725
INDIAN HEALTH FACILITIES	87	89	65	66	69	51	66	37	13	3
PREVENTIVE HEALTH SERVICES	160	165	169	201	214	210	277	278	277	277
ALCOHOL, DRUG ABUSE, MENTAL HEALTH SERVICES	128	172	69	90	107	70	22	43	34	27
OTHER HEALTH SERVICES	369	412	247	198	143	144	167	163	162	169
PREVENTIVE HEALTH SERVICES BLOCK GRANT[a]	194	118	126	107	89	96	85	88	89	89
ALCOHOL, DRUG ABUSE, MENTAL HEALTH BLOCK GRANT[a]	708	664	656	506	501	486	471	485	490	490
PRIMARY CARE BLOCK GRANT[a]	484	532	539	433	575	576	600	565	565	565
MATERNAL AND CHILD HEALTH BLOCK GRANT[a]	361	398	516	427	407	404	490	473	478	478
TOTAL--HEALTH SERVICES	3350	3446	3408	2960	3046	3102	3140	2907	2966	2948
TOTAL--HEALTH	53020	63690	72207	79877	87037	98407	103015	105903	114983	125300

APPENDIX C (cont.)

CURRENT DOLLARS

INCOME ASSISTANCE PROGRAMS	ENACTED						EST.	PROPOSED		
	FY 1980	FY 1981	FY 1982	FY 1983	FY 1984	FY 1985	FY 1986	FY 1987	FY 1988	FY 1989
HOUSING ASSISTANCE SUBAREA										
FARM LABOR HOUSING	13	17	20	16	11	3	10	12	11	8
MUTUAL AND SELF-HELP HOUSING	6	7	8	7	8	8	7	8	4	3
NONPROFIT SPONSOR HOUSING ASSISTANCE	0	0	0	0	0	0	0	0	-1	0
SUBSIDIZED HOUSING[f]	4529	5747	6880	7786	8774	9994	10642	10580	11006	11499
OTHER HOUSING[f]	932	1094	1156	1636	1255	1320	1535	1448	1433	1481
TOTAL--HOUSING ASSISTANCE	5480	6865	8064	9445	10048	11325	12194	12048	12453	12991
CASH ASSISTANCE SUBAREA										
SUPPLEMENTAL SECURITY INCOME	6411	7192	7677	8724	8498	9606	10162	10535	11742	11324
AID TO FAMILIES WITH DEPENDENT CHILDREN	7045	8176	7990	8392	8855	9224	9738	8933	9790	10044
EARNED INCOME TAX CREDIT	1275	1318	1201	1213	1193	1100	1283	1228	1112	1075
TOTAL--CASH ASSISTANCE	14731	16686	16868	18329	18546	19930	21183	20696	22644	22443
FOOD ASSISTANCE SUBAREA										
FOOD STAMPS	9117	11253	11014	12653	12375	12526	12488	12329	12693	12942
WOMEN, INFANTS, CHILDREN FOOD SUPPLEMENTS	717	930	930	1150	1398	1538	1618	1652	1669	1731
CHILD AND OTHER NUTRITION	4181	4019	3637	4069	4223	4407	4536	4113	4338	4607
TOTAL--FOOD ASSISTANCE	14015	16202	15581	17872	17996	18471	18642	18094	18700	19280
OTHER INCOME ASSISTANCE SUBAREA										
REFUGEE ASSISTANCE	368	726	1011	524	602	442	393	343	368	345
LOW INCOME ENERGY ASSISTANCE	1577	1780	1687	1993	2026	2141	2019	2091	2100	2100
OTHER INCOME ASSISTANCE	223	202	187	234	243	193	163	144	139	140
TOTAL--OTHER INCOME ASSISTANCE	2168	2708	2885	2751	2871	2776	2575	2578	2607	2585
TOTAL--INCOME ASSISTANCE	36394	42461	43398	48397	49461	52502	54594	53416	56404	57299

APPENDIX C (cont.)

CURRENT DOLLARS

	ENACTED						EST.	PROPOSED		
FOREIGN AID PROGRAMS	FY 1980	FY 1981	FY 1982	FY 1983	FY 1984	FY 1985	FY 1986	FY 1987	FY 1988	FY 1989
AGENCY FOR INTERNATIONAL DEVELOPMENT	1428	1544	1507	1657	1779	1929	2093	2084	2081	2075
MULTILATERAL DEVELOPMENT BANKS	784	955	1063	1242	1391	1427	1189	1574	1565	1353
PUBLIC LAW 480 FOOD ASSISTANCE	1073	1254	929	992	1085	1715	1373	1158	1175	1192
PEACE CORPS	101	99	103	110	111	118	123	126	126	129
ECONOMIC SUPPORT AND PEACEKEEPING	1904	2082	2441	2721	2913	4926	4852	4095	4330	4268
REFUGEE ASSISTANCE	446	384	382	319	336	385	343	340	345	334
INTERNATIONAL ORGANIZATIONS AND CONFERENCES	492	441	544	482	580	540	514	487	471	482
FOREIGN INFORMATION AND EXCHANGE	534	525	571	602	682	793	931	1043	1120	1220
OTHER INTERNATIONAL DEVELOPMENT ASSISTANCE	182	264	175	122	219	259	255	187	160	158
TOTAL--FOREIGN AID	6944	7548	7715	8247	9096	12092	11673	11094	11373	11211
ARTS AND CULTURE PROGRAMS										
CORPORATION FOR PUBLIC BROADCASTING	152	162	172	137	138	150	160	200	170	130
NATIONAL ENDOWMENT FOR THE ARTS	152	149	134	126	145	149	173	162	148	145
NATIONAL ENDOWMENT FOR THE HUMANITIES	168	166	137	134	140	150	148	130	127	127
SMITHSONIAN AND OTHER INSTITUTIONS	160	186	193	216	211	227	239	258	264	262
INSTITUTE OF MUSEUM SERVICES	13	0	28	9	17	19	26	16	0	0
TOTAL--ARTS AND CULTURE	645	663	664	622	651	695	746	766	709	664
ENVIRONMENT AND CONSERVATION PROGRAMS										
URBAN PARK AND RECREATION GRANTS	4	18	32	28	38	44	14	4	1	0
YOUTH CONSERVATION CORPS	60	27	6	0	0	0	0	0	0	0
FEDERAL LAND ACQUISITION	595	495	349	330	315	351	262	196	72	63
HISTORIC PRESERVATION FUND	49	53	37	31	51	29	18	3	2	0
TOTAL--ENVIRONMENT AND CONSERVATION	708	593	424	389	404	424	294	203	75	63
OTHER PROGRAMS										
NONPROFIT MAIL SUBSIDY[g]	276	298	270	274	297	346	296	0	0	0
OTHER MAIL SUBSIDY[h]	477	542	460	463	479	572	453	0	0	0
TOTAL--OTHER	753	840	730	737	776	918	749	0	0	0
GRAND TOTAL--ALL PROGRAMS	151894	171095	173681	184639	194026	214329	220885	215531	225227	234930

APPENDIX C (cont.)

Source: U.S. Office of Management and Budget, Budget of the United States Government, FY 1987 and preceding years, unpublished backup material; and other unpublished executive branch agency and Congressional budget material.

a. The current program was created by the Omnibus Budget Reconciliation Act of 1981. Outlay figures include spending for preexisting programs which covered the same activities.

b. The Job Training Partnership Act (JTPA) replaced the Comprehensive Employment and Training Act (CETA) in 1982.

c. Outlay figures do not include the effects of the enacted or proposed sale of loan assets.

d. Included in research and development outlays is the federal spending on research and development which goes outside the government to public and private, nonprofit colleges and universities and nonprofit research institutes. Intramural government spending and support going to for-profit businesses are not included.

e. Excludes revenues from Medicare premiums and collections.

f. Outlay figures exclude outlays in the public housing loan account and related proposed outlays in the subsidized housing account.

g. Outlay figures include the estimated Treasury subsidy for reduced mail rates for private, nonprofit organizations. The President's FY 1987 budget proposes to end the Treasury reimbursement to the Postal Service for subsidized mail rates, although the budget indicates that legislation will be proposed to allow the Postal Service to continue the subsidy on its own.

h. Outlay figures include the estimated Treasury subsidy for reduced mail rates for public, for-profit, and religious organizations. Also see note g.

APPENDIX D

THE URBAN INSTITUTE NONPROFIT SECTOR PROJECT PUBLICATIONS

In June 1982 The Urban Institute launched a major, multi-year project to examine the scope and operations of the private, nonprofit sector in the United States, and to assess the impact on nonprofit organizations and those they serve of recent changes in public policy. This project is directed by Dr. Lester M. Salamon and is supported by numerous corporations, community foundations, and national foundations. It involves work at the national level and in sixteen local areas throughout the country. The aim of this effort is to help nonprofit and philanthropic organizations cope with the major changes in public policy and economic circumstances under way in our nation, and to provide a solid factual basis for the decisions now being made about the appropriate roles of government, nonprofit organizations, and businesses in serving community needs.

In each community where this work is proceeding, two main kinds of research and reports are being produced. One involves analysis of federal, state, and local government spending on programs of concern to nonprofit organizations, and of the extent of government reliance on nonprofits to deliver human services. The other involves surveys of nonprofit agencies themselves, showing the sector's size, scope and character, sources of funds, and responses to government retrenchment.

Local research sites include:

Atlanta	Minneapolis/St. Paul
Boise	New York City
Chicago	Phoenix
Dallas/Fort Worth	Pittsburgh
Flint	Rhode Island
Jackson	San Francisco

In addition to its series of local reports, the project is producing a number of reports that place its findings in a national context. The following list presents all project publications to date as of May, 1986, and describes how to obtain publications. For further information on this project, contact: Clarke Maylone, The Urban Institute, 2100 M Street, N.W., Washington, D.C. 20037, 202/857-8620.

PROJECT PUBLICATIONS: MAY 1986

A. National Publications

"Partners in Public Service: Government and the Nonprofit Sector in the American Welfare State," by Lester M. Salamon, James C. Musselwhite, Jr., and Carol J. De Vita, paper presented at the 1986 Spring Research Forum of the Independent Sector, New York, NY (1986) ($2.75).

"Government and the Voluntary Sector in an Era of Retrenchment: The American Experience," by Lester M. Salamon, Journal of Public Policy, 1986.

"Partners in Public Service: Toward a Theory of Government-Nonprofit Relations," by Lester M. Salamon, paper presented at the Annual Meeting of the Society for the Study of Social Problems, Washington, D.C., (1985) ($4.00).

"New Federalism and the Nonprofit Sector," by James C. Musselwhite, Jr., paper presented at the Annual Meeting of the American Political Science Association, New Orleans, (1985) ($2.50).

"Social Welfare Policy and Privatization: Theory and Reality in Policymaking," by James C. Musselwhite, Jr. and Lester M. Salamon, in Mark S. Rosentraub (ed.), Urban Policy Choices: Theory and Prescription in an Era of Uncertain Resources, (New York: Praeger, forthcoming 1986); paper available from The Urban Institute ($2.50).

"Nonprofits and the Federal Budget: Deeper Cuts Ahead," by Lester M. Salamon and Alan J. Abramson, Foundation News, April (1985) ($1.00).

Child-Serving Nonprofit Organizations in an Era of Government Retrenchment, by Madeleine H. Kimmich, Michael Gutowski, and Lester M. Salamon, (Washington, D.C.: The Urban Institute, 1985) ($7.75).

"The Invisible Partnership: Government and the Nonprofit Sector," by Lester M. Salamon, Bell Atlantic Quarterly, Autumn 1984 ($1.00).

"Nonprofit Organizations: The Lost Opportunity," by Lester M. Salamon, in John Palmer and Isabel Sawhill, eds., The Reagan Record (Cambridge: Ballinger Publishing Company, 1984) ($12.95).

"Religious Congregations as Social Service Agencies: How Extensive Are They?", by Lester M. Salamon and Fred Teitelbaum, Foundation News, September/October, (1984) ($1.00).

"Nonprofits: The Results Are Coming In," by Lester M. Salamon, Foundation News, August (1984) ($1.00).

"Voluntary Organizations and the Crisis of the Welfare State," by Lester M. Salamon, James C. Musselwhite, Jr., and Alan J. Abramson, New England Journal of Human Services, Winter 1984, Volume IV. ($3.50).

"Families in Crisis: The Capacity of Private Nonprofit Agencies to Respond," testimony of Lester M. Salamon, U.S. Congress, Select Committee on Children, Youth and Families, Hearing, 98 Cong., 1 sess. (1983) ($3.00).

"The New Federalism, the Federal Budget, and the Nonprofit Sector," testimony of Lester M. Salamon, U.S. Congress, Joint Economic Committee, Hearing on "New Federalism: Its Impact on the Private, Nonprofit Sector," 98 Cong., 1 sess. (1983) ($3.00).

"The Nonprofit Sector," by Lester M. Salamon and Alan J. Abramson, in John Palmer and Isabel Sawhill, eds., The Reagan Experiment (Washington, D.C.: The Urban Institute Press, 1982). ($12.95).

"The Impact of the 1981 Tax Act on Individual Charitable Giving," by Charles T. Clotfelter and Lester M. Salamon, National Tax Journal, (June 1982) ($5.00).

The Federal Budget and the Nonprofit Sector, by Lester M. Salamon and Alan J. Abramson, (Washington, D.C.: The Urban Institute Press, 1982) ($11.50).

B. Local Research Site Reports

Atlanta

Government Spending and the Nonprofit Sector in Atlanta/Fulton County, by James C. Musselwhite, Jr., Winsome Hawkins, and Lester M. Salamon, (Washington, D.C.: The Urban Institute Press, 1985) ($12.95).

The Atlanta Nonprofit Sector in a Time of Government Retrenchment, by Paul C. Lippert, Michael Gutowski, and Lester M. Salamon (Washington, D.C.: The Urban Institute Press, 1984) ($12.95).

Boise

The Boise Nonprofit Sector in a Time of Government Retrenchment, by David A. Johnson and David M. Altschuler, (Washington, D.C.: an Urban Institute Research Report, 1986) ($12.95).

Government Spending and the Nonprofit Sector in Boise/Ada County, Idaho, by David A. Johnson and James C. Musselwhite, Jr., (Washington, D.C.: an Urban Institute Research Report, 1985) ($12.95).

Chicago

The Chicago Nonprofit Sector in a Time of Government Retrenchment, by Kirsten A. Gronbjerg, Lester M. Salamon, and Michael Gutowski, (Washington, D.C.: The Urban Institute Press, 1985) ($12.95).

Government Spending and the Nonprofit Sector in Cook County/Chicago, by Kirsten A. Gronbjerg, James C. Musselwhite, Jr., and Lester M. Salamon, (Washington, D.C.: The Urban Institute Press, 1984) ($12.95).

Dallas-Fort Worth

The Dallas/Fort Worth Nonprofit Sector in a Time of Government Retrenchment, by Carol J. De Vita and Lester M. Salamon (Washington, D.C.: an Urban Institute Research Report, 1986) ($12.95).

Government Spending and the Nonprofit Sector in Dallas, by Mark S. Rosentraub, James C. Musselwhite, Jr., and Lester M. Salamon (Washington, D.C.: an Urban Institute Research Report, 1985) ($12.95).

Flint Michigan

Government Spending and the Nonprofit Sector in Two Michigan Communities: Flint/Genesee County and Tuscola County, by James C. Musselwhite, Jr., and Lauren K. Saunders (Washington, D.C.: The Urban Institute Press, 1985) ($12.95).

Jackson, Mississippi

The Jackson Nonprofit Sector in a Time of Government Retrenchment, by Stephen L. Rozman, Carol J. De Vita, and Lester M. Salamon, (Washington, D.C.: an Urban Institute Research Report, 1986) ($12.95).

Government Spending and the Nonprofit Sector in Two Mississippi Communities: Jackson/Hinds County and Vicksburg/Warren County, by Stephen L. Rozman and James C. Musselwhite, Jr., (Washington, D.C.: an Urban Institute Research Report, 1985) ($12.95).

Minneapolis-St. Paul

Government Spending and the Nonprofit Sector in Minneapolis/Hennepin County, Minnesota, by Lori E. Marczak, James C. Musselwhite, Jr., and Wolfgang Bielefeld (Washington, D.C.: an Urban Institute Research Report, 1985) ($12.95).

Government Spending and the Nonprofit Sector in St. Paul/Ramsey County, Minnesota, by Barbara L. Lukermann, James C. Musselwhite, Jr., and Lori E. Marczak (Washington, D.C.: an Urban Institute Research Report, 1985) ($12.95).

The Twin Cities Nonprofit Sector in a Time of Government Retrenchment, by Barbara Lukermann, Madeleine Kimmich, and Lester M. Salamon (Washington, D.C.: The Urban Institute Press, 1984) ($12.95).

Phoenix

The Phoenix Nonprofit Sector in a Time of Government Retrenchment, by Annie Millar, Carol J. De Vita, Lester M. Salamon, and John S. Hall (Washington, D.C.: an Urban Institute Research Report, 1986) ($12.95).

Government Spending and the Nonprofit Sector in Two Arizona Communities: Phoenix/Maricopa County and Pinal County, by John S. Hall, James C. Musselwhite, Jr., Lori E. Marczak, and David Alteide (Washington, D.C.: an Urban Institute Research Report, 1985) ($12.95).

Pittsburgh

Government Spending and the Nonprofit Sector in Pittsburgh/Allegheny County, by James C. Musselwhite, Jr., Rosalyn B. Katz, and Lester M. Salamon (Washington, D.C.: The Urban Institute Press, 1985) ($12.95)

The Pittsburgh Nonprofit Sector in a Time of Government Retrenchment, by Michael Gutowski, Lester M. Salamon, and Karen Pittman (Washington, D.C.: The Urban Institute Press, 1984) ($12.95).

Providence, Rhode Island

Partners in Public Service: Government and the Nonprofit Sector in Rhode Island, by Diane Disney, Madeleine Kimmich, and James C. Musselwhite, Jr., (Washington, D.C.: The Urban Institute Press, 1984) ($14.95).

San Francisco

The San Francisco Bay Area Nonprofit Sector in a Time of Government Retrenchment, by Paul Harder, Madeleine Kimmich, and Lester M. Salamon, (Washington, D.C.: The Urban Institute Press, 1985) ($12.95).

Government Spending and the Nonprofit Sector in San Francisco, by Paul Harder, James C. Musselwhite, Jr., and Lester M. Salamon (Washington, D.C.: The Urban Institute Press, 1984) ($12.95).

C. How to Obtain Publications

1. All publications of The Urban Institute Press can be obtained from the Press at: P.O. Box 19958, Hampaen Station, Baltimore, MD 21211 (301)338-6951. To the prices shown add $2.00 for postage and handling. Payment can be by purchase order, prepayment, or Visa/Mastercard.

2. Publications listed above that are not published by The Urban Institute Press are available, at prices shown, from: The Urban Institute, Library Information Clearinghouse, P. O. Box 7273, Dept. C, Washington, D.C. 20044 (202) 857-8688. Prepayment is required, and there is a postage and handling charge of $2.00 at minimum or 15 percent of the total purchase.

3. The Reagan Record is available in local bookstores, or from Ballinger Publishing Company, Cambridge, Mass.